The Gift of Ben

The Gift of Ben

Loving through Imperfection

Lindsey Rogers-Seitz

Wellness Writers Press

WELLNESS WRITERS PRESS
Published by Pure Ink Press
Middletown, MD

Copyright © 2023 by Lindsey Rogers-Seitz
All rights reserved.

No part of this publication may be reproduced, stored in a retrieval system, or transmitted in any form or by any means, electronic, mechanical, photocopying, recording, or otherwise, without the prior written permission of the author.

This book is sold with the understanding that neither the author nor the publisher are rendering any form of advice, and is based solely upon the author's personal experience. Any form of physical, emotional, or mental health concerns should be addressed directly to a professional. The author and/or publisher shall have neither liability nor responsibility to any person or entity with respect to any loss or damage caused, or alleged to be caused, directly or indirectly by the information contained in this book.

Paperback ISBN: 979-8-9876015-0-1
Hardcover ISBN: 979-8-9876015-3-2
Ebook ISBN: 979-8-9876015-7-0

Library of Congress Control Number: 2023934367

Cover design by Nikola Tikoski
Cover photograph by Kristijan Sekulic

wellnesswriterspress.com
www.pureinkpress.com

For Ben

DISCLAIMER

The events and people portrayed in this book are real. I relied on my memory and conversations with individuals involved in the depicted events to recreate them as truthfully as possible. When available, sources other than my memory were used to verify facts, such as journals, official records, photographs, transcripts, emails, and articles. Some events are presented outside of their chronological order, while others from different times are combined into one scene or dialogue. To protect the privacy of individuals involved, some descriptions, names, and other details have been changed.

Juvenile court proceedings and information from Connecticut State Department of Children and Families (DCF) investigations are held confidential under state law in order to protect the privacy of juveniles involved. I tried to only include portions of our investigation that lent themselves to the furtherance of the greater story of the book. I have purposefully changed names where appropriate and removed many of the private discussions that took place off the record between me or my attorney and third parties within or affiliated with DCF or other governmental departments in order to protect the anonymity and career integrity of those involved. I have excluded certain private details in the best interests of my children as well as any events or comments that are either irrelevant, inaccurate, unsubstantiated by facts, or defamatory in nature.

"The universe is wider than our views of it."
— HENRY DAVID THOREAU

Prologue

I did not break the moment I found out my son had died. I did not even break within the week or month. It was a much slower process than that. A meticulous unraveling. I had struggled with mental illness for nearly a third of my life, so I saw it coming. You would think I could have done something to prevent it, but life is not always that simple. After the final break, I found myself sitting alone beneath a golden aspen in the mountains of Colorado. As I began writing, the words that flowed surprised me. I had run away from the world for the last time and was finally setting myself free.

I thought back to the night we found out we were having a baby boy. As darkness fell in Ridgefield, Connecticut, my two daughters had sat on our couch, legs crossed, anxious, waiting to hear whether the new baby would be a boy or girl. Kaylyn, my oldest, held the manila envelope in her hands. I had asked the ultrasound technician to handwrite the sex on a slip of paper. We would open it together as a family. My husband, Kyle, and I sat across from them on the love seat, anxious too. Kaylyn ripped the envelope open, jerking the paper out with a rush of excitement. She held it up, examining the cursive writing. "It's a..." she paused, "*boy!*" I watched Kyle's eyes expand to the size of golf balls with excitement. I was scared. I did not know how to raise a boy and was unsure of how to love a boy. I did not know at the time that Ben would show me not only how to love him but how to love myself. His passion was infectious.

He died when he was fifteen months old, on a sweltering hot day in July of 2014.

Kyle forgot to take him to daycare that morning. He passed away in the car, sitting in the parking lot of my husband's office. I miss him, oh how I miss him. No book could convey the depth of a mother's longing. But I discovered on that chilly fall day in Aspen that this book was not meant to be about grief and loss. It was meant to be about the love and hope I found on the other side of broken. I had lived in the darkness for too long, afraid to be who I really was, to admit one of the most integral parts of my life and say to another person, "I have a mental illness. Let me tell you about it." Ben did more than love me and fill my life with joy; he brought me back to myself, and that is the love of a son for his mother. His life taught me that what exists when nothing else is left is pure love, passionate and gritty. He made me see the light.

I know telling my story could have many ramifications. I fear I may no longer be accepted in the legal community or by other parents or friends, as many will not understand. But there is no other way for this memoir to be written. It is structured in short scenes of raw emotion and description, and I have taken poetic license in sentence structure and cadence throughout, as these were effective methods for relaying my state of mind, emotions, and intellectual journey. In the crisp fall air of Colorado in 2015, this approach was the only way the words would flow. This is my story, and I have to be true to myself for the first time. I want to say the things others rarely do, to delve into the human part of us all. The messy, imperfect part we keep hidden deep within us—that which makes us truly beautiful. This book is meant not only for those struggling with difficulties in life, grief, and loss, but also for those who have lived in the darkness for too long. Look up and you will see the light. You are not alone; we are all around you.

PART ONE

1

September 17, 2015
Colorado

My body is lead; I am glued to the ground. I am becoming the ground and the stucco wall behind me. It is scratching my back. I am lost. I am somewhere. I am nowhere, and I cannot tell anyone where or how to find me. I think maybe if I just sit long enough, I will come full circle and find myself.

I try to move my feet, but they remain anchored, unmoving. I try to keep my hair out of my face as I bend over, but it's useless so I give up. Gravity pulls my fingers back to the rocks below me. I prop myself up. There is only the nonsense of an infinity of time and distance through which I have come undone.

I breathe and rest my head against the wall. I am so tired of running, so tired of hiding. There is only darkness, a small bush in front of me. No cars. I am finally alone. I have fallen to the ground against this stucco wall, expecting to crash through another layer of myself, but I have hit the ground beneath me with a grunt. I dig my fingers into the earth. This is the bottom. There is nowhere else to go except beneath the ground, and I am not ready for that.

My head is spinning. I begin to shiver and stare into the night sky, broken only by sporadic streetlights. I have long wondered what would exist when nothing else was left. I have found out. There is the blackness of the night, a chill, and the sound of my breath. Waiting to be found. Waiting for the impossible.

I hear a car. I cannot move. I am useless. The car parks and Kyle steps out. I am found, and I am relieved. He pulls my arm, but I do not budge. I remain glued. He puts his weight behind me and tries to lift using both arms as leverage. I stand, wobbling, so he helps me walk to the car. Driving away from the bar, I hear voices beside me in the back seat. "Someone drugged her drink." I can hear no more. I lie back against the leather, watching the blur of the city pass by. It is too cold. I curl up into a ball.

After some time passes, I see our house. I remember our sitter and ask to be left inside the car. Kyle returns after she exits. I am brought in. There is a bed. It is my bed, and I am so happy to be home. I collapse on the comforter and ask him to just lie with me. He complies.

I continue to shiver. Then I cry. "I don't even know who I am anymore," I tell him. "My soul is being torn apart from the inside out." There is a pain that I am trying to explain, but I cannot gather my words.

"Can we get under the covers?" he asks as I begin to doze off.

"No," I mumble and pull him tighter.

"I'm cold," he says again, after what seems like hours. I finally relent. I allow my mind to return to the darkness.

It is morning. The girls are getting out of the car, running toward the school. I feel as if my life is carried with them; as if I am being sucked backward into myself with the rush forward of their movement. Their book bags jostle as they run. I am driving to nowhere. I pick up the phone. I set it down. It is like it used to be. The synapses in my brain are too quick and out of order. There is a frenzy of activity, but nothing comes of it. Only flashes of lightning bursting here and there inside my head, but going nowhere. No thoughts form. I keep driving. I am frantic and cannot sit still. My body is alive with energy.

I am searching for a room with four walls and barred windows. I do not find what I am looking for. I dial a number. No sentences come. I can go away, far away from here and this nothingness of me. I leave a message with my psychiatrist. "Come see me. Come see me soon," she urges when she returns my call. I want to run again, but I am so tired. I am tired of running. There is nowhere deeper to go, nowhere else to fall. No one to catch me. I must catch myself.

I am sitting in her office, talking. I talk so quickly, yet there is nothing to say. Just the pain. "The pain," I tell her. Of me and who I am not, or who I am but not willing to accept. She hands me a prescription as I relent. I will try one last time.

It is now nighttime; the house is quiet. My mind is quiet now too. I see a circle of powdery white resting on my tongue. I taste the bitterness as it begins to dissolve and I swallow. I continue to look in the mirror but do not see myself. I see nothing. It is all gone, and now I must rebuild. I will have to go back, so far back, and there will be many pieces. But I will find them, one by one. I will begin tomorrow; for tonight, I must rest.

2

Monday, July 7, 2014
Connecticut

He was here, and then he was nowhere.

I had cut through the silence that hung in the room, thick and precipitous. I read the truth in the angst of their wide eyes staring back at me, interspersed within the blur of white hospital coats. The amorphous mass shifted uncomfortably, as if waiting for something. I had missed the introductions, so I focused in on the young nurse standing in front of the door. She appeared to be there by happenstance, and it gave me comfort. Her eyes were red, which seemed appropriate. The man with the glasses and clipboard started talking. I watched his mouth move; I heard only the shifting of the Earth beneath my feet.

My mind fell out of itself when I finally heard the words "He didn't make it." It had begun to falter early on, piecing together the scraps of a failing world, but it had been the walk down the hallway where the living lay, to the small room (*This is where they tell people,* I had thought) with a black Bible on a circular table, that had caused my brain to finally clamp shut in order to stop the bleeding.

I sensed their breath levitating, paused midair, waiting for the break to occur. Time became what it was meant to be—unmoving. The world around me, four walls and a mass of white, disappeared, and I was inside myself, a pool of darkness, infinite time, and a calm. So much calm. I sensed a shedding of my outer body, leaving nothing behind. Just the essence of me. Every moment of my life flashed before my eyes and coalesced into one, still and silent. The nowhere he was supposed to be turned into the everywhere I really was. With an inward gasp—"oh my God, no, no"—reality became me and hands covering my mouth, head hung low. *Is this what the black book on the circular table means by born again?*

Kyle is dead, I thought. *He's killed himself. I've lost two people in one day.* "Where's my husband?" My eyes move from the floor to the nebulous mass, ebbing and flowing with uncertainty.

"He's in a room," someone answered.

I pictured him lying supine, clear coiled tubes running from his mouth, or dead. He was just simply dead. "How is he?" I finally asked.

They paused and looked at each other, until one responded, "Well, he's... despondent. Do you want to see him?"

The question confused me. *Why would I not want to see him?* I thought.

"Yes. Right now."

The mass shrank in size, as a silent breath of anxiety was exorcised from its body. I stared at them as if they were missing something integral. I had just become unbroken. I had finally understood. I had always been, and forever would be, loving and losing Ben in this one moment that simply Is.

3

Fall 2002

It had begun years ago. I had built these walls of me. Cement bricks, shiny mustard-colored, slick to the touch. I sat on a wooden bench protruding from the wall itself. It was part of me too, I presumed. Existing there was a comfortable acquiescence. The small, square window framed by the door allowed the others to remain unseen. I was the observed.

I began to pace the floors of the eight-by-twelve-foot room, hoping the movement would separate my thoughts, which were entwined, of where I was and how I had gotten here. When the door finally opened, a young resident walked in with dark brown hair and round wire-rimmed glasses. An air of reticence followed him into the room. He offered his hand as I stopped pacing to comply with the formality.

"Tell me, why are you here, Mrs. Seitz?"

It just happened; one day I simply came unfurled. It was a dark fog with jagged edges, not like I had expected it to be. They irritated me, causing a blood-borne agitation. It had spread to my bones, and I would excise it if I had to.

The pills had rattled in my purse. They would perform when asked, but for some weeks now had served only as an accompaniment. I had confessed my indiscretions once, and they had prayed for me. The pills still jostled in my purse as I walked out of the church. I would pray too, I had promised them. None of it made sense. I was young, newly married.

"I don't understand what's happening to me." I looked at him, pausing for an explanation. None came. "I'm happy."

"Do you want to hurt yourself?" he inquired further.

"I don't want to, no, that's why I brought myself here. You need to help me," I responded. Here I was safe.

The psychiatrist on-call was a female, sandy blonde hair hanging over her shoulders. She had joined the discussion and sat in a chair watching me.

"Why are you here, Mrs. Seitz?"

"I don't know."

"We can't keep you unless you are a threat to yourself or others."

"You've got to keep me safe." I ran my hands through my hair. My muscles were alive with energy. My body squirmed like a trapped animal, relaying a message that my words could not convey.

Something is wrong. Make it stop. God, please help me, it spoke.

4

The female doctor led the procession down the hallway. She wore high heels. I heard only the cadence of formality. As we approached the double doors, I wanted to turn and run, as if by reversing course I could reverse time. I held my breath, retaining the stale air of history.

I had been tracing the patterned floor as I walked. My mind focused in on the simplicity of its symmetry. Black lines passed in a blur. They ushered me into a hallway of empty rooms, closed off by doors on each end. The new mass of white that had been loitering silently in the hallway scattered as we entered. The mother had arrived. A hand guided me into the first room on the left, but I knew where to find my husband. The sounds were unmistakable. I felt a faltering expectation around me. I was supposed to look at him.

I was not sure at the time what I was witnessing. A body torn asunder by love and longing. A specter of the man I had once known, an empty vessel with no purpose except to breathe. It was the complete degeneration of a human into a form of near nonexistence.

As I watched the scene unfold before me, I was left questioning what it meant to love another. Do they become a part of you, such that when they are gone, a part of you leaves too? Do souls become intertwined, with the distance of one from another causing physical pain? I understood instantaneously—that which we call love is much more than an emotion. It is too integral to be merely that.

I did not get the chance to say goodbye, I thought as I stared at him. He would never be the same. Our life was over and I missed him already. Part of him had died, and only a primal grief remained. His mind had fled long ago, as a refugee into the night. The gravity of longing was already taking its physical toll. He sat on the edge of the gurney, stripped down to an undershirt, khaki pants, and brown socks. His body rocked toward me. Then away. Red face, veins bulging, salty remains of sweat already forming streaks across his face. The reality of death crawled like ants all over his body, as one foot traveled up the opposite leg, trying to scrape them off.

Nurses and police stood in the hallway. No one could watch these events unfold. It was the pain from which you turn your head, and I wanted them to turn away. Please don't watch this. There was something personal about the night, something I needed to keep private. I remained frozen in the doorway, trying to read his emotions through his body. I heard only the nonsensical mutterings of mourning.

"No, no, no, this is not real," he mumbled with each thrust of his hands against his head, then moving down his body and back up again. His head shook with each repetition of the phrase, as if to oust an intruder. The reality of this day. He was, as I had been while seated in the room with the black book on the circular table, alone. I could not save him. I could not take the pain away. I was helpless.

Love transcended itself without my knowing, and I became him, inside of him. I was the pain languishing inside his soul. He would have to extricate me from the inside out. My body moved intimately, as I climbed onto his lap, straddling his body with my legs, wrapping my fingers between his as I tried to remove them from the skin of his face.

"I love you. I love you. I love you."

He continued rocking.

"Look at me," I said again and again. "I love you. Put your arms around me."

"No, no, no, this is not real," he repeated.

"Put. Your arms. Around me. I'm here."

His mumbling broke into screaming sobs, as if the release of one body into another was physically painful. My shoulder became wet with tears as he squeezed my body until I hurt. There was another kind of hurt boiling inside of me too, and after several minutes, thoughts overcame my initial instinct. I did not understand why my body had responded like that, why I had told him I loved him. *He doesn't get to sob,* I thought. *To touch me. To rely on me to save him.* These arms held Ben this morning. I could not save or pity him. I only wanted him to suffer, as my skin began to recoil from his touch.

"I love you and I'm here, but I need some time to myself. I'll be back."

"Don't leave," he cried. *Leave* was an ambiguous word.

"I have to," I replied as I stood to walk away. My brain swam in the icy waters of grief and shock. I became numb. I understood nothing. He had killed Ben, yet I had told him I loved him. I had not thought it through, or maybe that was love itself.

As I left the room, I leaned in to whisper to the nurse standing guard, "Have you given him anything?"

"Not yet," he responded.

"You need to give him something to calm him down. Because he is *not* okay. He can't get through this without medication."

I could not get through this if I were him. *Thank God it's not me,* I thought in a moment of weakness as I walked out of the room.

5

I sifted through the ruins only momentarily. They were unrecognizable. We would have to build anew, something stronger and more real, or else we would have to just walk away from each other, from life. As I took my seat in one of the blue plastic chairs lining the hallway, I noticed a new sensation growing in my chest. The pain born from a heart existing outside the body. It was not even a heart. It was more. It was part of Ben, and Ben was gone. It had torn through the fabric of space and time, was floating aimlessly in another world, already searching for something it could no longer have. As I sat in silence, I knew. That was what it meant to love another.

I looked around me, as if in anticipation of something imminent. Staff were milling about, standing and talking, watching. As shock began to set in, thoughts returned, matching my racing pulse. The instinct of fight or flight was being born, and as my mind began to pick up speed, I allowed it. I needed it to fill the void where my heart once existed. I fumbled with my phone, then stared. I felt I needed to say something, to add words to the silence, which was unbearable.

"I can't cry. Don't take this as anything meaningful. I must be in shock or something. I don't know what to say."

"We know," someone murmured.

During this first phase, sitting stiffly in the chair while the others tried not to look out of respect, my mind began to careen out of control. Before this day, I had found empowerment in independence. I saw a weakness in needing others, but I had been wrong.

"I need Michele. I need someone here," I said aloud to no one, possibly just to recognize the words aloud. *I need someone to translate these words and events for me,* I thought. A foreign language was being spoken, and my glances around the hallway showed red eyes, whispers, police, strangers entering, exiting. The sounds of moans coming from my husband's room. I could translate none of these signals.

"Here, we'll get you a room so you can be alone and talk," a voice asserted.

Nothing makes sense; please translate.

The curtain was drawn, and I stepped in. I heard the swish of privacy close behind me. Lights were switched on. The starkness was an overwhelming reality. "I can't handle the brightness," I muttered. The nurse walked in quick obedience to switch the back dimmer lights on and then left. My nervous system eased slightly. I felt as if I could finally hide, and as the room opened its mouth of darkness to me, I visualized another room where my son lay. My mind convulsed, began to sputter and moan.

He didn't make it. Left in car. Forgot. Daycare.

Starkness of bright lights.

Police and red eyes of disbelief surrounding me.

I touched his skin this morning, but now he's gone. With that thought I faltered and began dialing, a selfish instinct, making me feel weak and dependent. It was an intimate, personal grief, and I feared for anyone to bear witness, as if by mere observance the pain would be transferred from my body to theirs. However, the burden was unbearable, and I thought I may just be able to survive if I could share it. I needed to find my way through the ruins.

So I called my dear friend, Michele. "I need you to come to the hospital. I can't talk about it right now, but please come. Something has happened to Ben."

We had sat together by the lake, watching, as he toddled through the sand, his toes curled under to steady himself. He squatted to trace tiny fingers through the sand, sensations of a new world, all his own. He gathered rocks, throwing them in amazement, turning toward us, golden tendrils, tinged with red in the light, falling into his eyes, a grin, as if to say, "Isn't this world stunning, Mama?" I looked at her, and we both smiled at each other, laughed, and then smiled back at him. Yes. Yes, it is.

When she appeared in the doorway, I felt an instantaneous relief. I was finally not alone. She had short blonde hair and tan skin from the summer we had all spent together and was my sense of a better place, the past, when we were happy. We had planned a summer vacation together, and in two weeks, in another world, there would be a little boy on the Cape, with a blonde-haired woman, building sand castles. There would be belly laughs and smiles. A glitter of blue eyes, and a mother would stand to the side taking pictures.

I still held onto the hope she would tell me it was all a dream. My mind was beginning to shift and lose steam. I needed her to translate quickly.

She rushed in and whispered, "Oh, honey," and hugged me.

"Did they tell you?" I asked. Because I could not say the words yet.

"Yes, they did."

My hands again were raised to my mouth, cupping the breath I would blow to the sky, to the moment that would be, on the beach, in another world. My head sank into her shoulders.

"Okay!" She gathered herself. "What can I do? Do you want me to call the pastor? Do you want to see your parents?"

I visualized them receiving the news, hysterics, a religion that had failed them, leaving nothing. "I want my parents here for support, but I can't see them yet. I can't see them cry. It will break me."

"Okay," she replied. "So I'll go ahead and call them at least." She paused. "Pastor Bill too?"

Is there even a God? I thought. As a young girl, I had sat in the pew, knock-knees showing below a flowered church dress, peering out from behind a hymnal. Southern sweat beaded on our foreheads as we sang "Amazing Grace." We finished fervently, "In the name of the Father, the Son, and the Holy Spirit. Amen." There were hands held high and a frantic energy, but during the calm a few moments before, there had only been silence. What did that mean? I was unsure what a pastor could do. For my truth was simply Ben was here and now he is nowhere.

"Yes, call him," I replied and collapsed on the bed.

6

He was my flame, as I was his, and this was the night the fire began to rage. The yearning was a deep torment. To be able to release my body into his, to relent and cry with him, to be a part of him, as I had always been. I knew his every fear, desire, I knew all of him. Yet that night we repelled each other, and a space remained between us where I dared not reach. I entered his room in fits, only long enough to satisfy my need to let him know I was there, to keep the wounds of his suffering from deepening. My skin became charred at the edges.

"If you stay with him, you will have to learn to live with two emotions at once. To just sit with them, let them exist, and move on," my therapist would tell me weeks later. She was referring to our Western way of thinking, of two-valued logic. If I hated him, I would have to leave him. If I loved him, I would stay. If I felt both, I must learn how to love him through it all, which had felt impossible that night, but I knew she was right. Eastern philosophers had long ago introduced a four-valued logic. I neither loved nor hated him. I loved and hated him. It was an emotion with no name, somewhere in between.

"He's asking for you," a nurse kept reminding me.

I don't care. I do care.

Make him suffer. Save him.

For hours I wavered between his bedside and solitude. He reached to hug me. He needed to hold me, to keep me there. So I let him, and my skin burned and blistered with the redness of anger, for in those moments I was being asked to reassure him of something I knew not. He continued to weep, soaked from sweat and tears.

A male nurse was present, watching us interact. Kyle spoke only in choppy words and phrases as his arms jerked back and forth between reaching for me as I pulled away, and covering his head, where reality boiled.

"But you… you are not going to be okay…. This will…," he trailed off. "You will leave… oh my God, Ben… the kids…."

"No, I'm going to take care of you. Just let me," I finally responded.

"But you…" as the crying returned, his body began swaying back and forth, veins bulging.

The nurse served as his rational brain, breaking in to tell him that I was okay. "Just let her be here for you. One day you will have to be there for her, just not today."

He already has been there for me, in my worst moments, I thought, and I pulled him closer, before the heat became too much to bear.

"I love you, but Ben is dead. I've got to go for now. I need time alone."

"No," he muttered and reached for me as I let his sweaty hands slide off my arm to escape the burning.

7

It was the carefree summer of 1998. He was twenty and I was nineteen. He was the friend of a friend, helping move boxes into my college apartment. Dark brown hair cut like a soldier, strong arms that could carry me if needed, deep hazel eyes, soft skin, a boyish tenor.

I had never had much need for men—too much to accomplish, not enough time to need anyone. Success would give me power, not another person, not reliance. I would one day be a lawyer in New York City, a boyfriend maybe, but no kids, no time. I found power in self-sufficiency.

Yet this one was different. We resonated profoundly, and I shied away. He was in school training to be an electrical engineer. I was sure he was already taken. His calm innocence drew me in, the *"yes, sir"* with a shy chuckle as he addressed my father, his tan and chiseled muscles, the downward slant of his face as he worked, carefully carrying my life inside the apartment with him, as if not to break any of its parts. He avoided eye contact and mindless chatter. He had a job to do.

When each box and piece of bedroom furniture had been placed inside, there was an exchange of *thank yous*, a bit of banter to fill the space, between us and time, when we would question our very existence together.

I watched as he waved goodbye.

8

Winter 2002

I stared into the darkness of the night sky as my husband drove. I needed to focus on something other than my racing mind, and the stars offered glimmers of hope. Yet when he turned onto the highway, my attention was immediately drawn back into reality. We were not going to get ice cream.

"Where are we going?" I asked. My voice began to escalate to match the rising agitation in my body and mind.

"I'm taking you to Duke. You are sick, and you need help," he responded calmly.

"No!" This time I was screaming. "I just want to be at home with you!" I lunged for the door, causing him to swerve onto the shoulder of the highway, instantly locking the doors to prevent my escape.

"Stop," he said firmly, grabbing my arm to keep me safe.

The car slowed as we exited the off ramp leading to Duke University Hospital in Durham, North Carolina, where he knew I would be kept safe. This was my chance, and I took it. In one motion, the door was unlocked and I grasped the seat belt to unbuckle. The door opened, and he swerved onto the shoulder, screaming for me to stop with his hand holding the seat belt in place. But my pain was not one that could be contained with the touch of a hand, so he began pulling into the closest parking lot, the door hanging open as he drove.

When his hold let up to reach for the parking brake, I lunged again, grabbed the door handle, and pushed violently. All but my legs were free, eyes fixed on a distant goal, a tree line, where I could flee and hide. His right hand grabbed my pants buckle and he pulled as I pushed, screaming to no avail. I saw his left hand reach for his phone, and I took the opportunity to kick and hit, fingers scratching at his face, anything I could reach. Primal instinct had overtaken me.

"I hate you. I only married you out of pity. I don't love you. Who do you think you are?" I yelled. If I cut him deeply enough, he would let me go, I assured myself. But when I realized my pain was no match for his strength and he would never let me go, I was relegated to sobs as he tied me down with his body against the side of the car door and dialed 911.

"I need help. I'm in a parking lot with my wife trying to get her to the hospital. She's manic depressive," he informed the dispatcher.

As I heard those words, only sobs escaped into the quiet of the night.

9

I had seen glimpses in his blue eyes. Of a journey. Of truth. They stunned me, shone through me. It was the deep blue of the sky where on a clear day I could see Heaven above and the waters below.[1] They were staring up at me the night he was born, holding a transcendent wisdom beyond his years. As I sat on the edge of the hospital bed the night he died, I could focus on nothing else. It was as if they were beckoning me until I relented and began to merge into their ocean blue, allowing the first undulations of shock to flow through my body like waves.

I was blind but knew there were faces in front of me, the same doctor with the heels, a cadence of formality, and the nurse from the room with the black book, on a circular table. Michele stood in the periphery.

"We need to ask you something." They stood close to me, making sure to look into my eyes, as if in preparation.

"Do you want to have time with him? To see him and say goodbye?"

Again, a shedding of my outer body, leaving nothing behind. A pool of darkness. I could think of no reality. There was no up, down, left, right, dead, alive. Only a gasp emitted, screaming in a whisper of cries: "I don't know. I don't know. What do I do? Someone help me!"

I thought of him with his green alligator pajamas and sleepy eyes that had been alive just that morning, curls falling over his face, which I had brushed, and the soft skin of his arm, which I had kissed. I wanted to remember that Ben. "What does he look like? Will I regret it? What do I do? Just tell me!"

I no longer heard her heels, and I sensed a pause. I am sure she could tell I was slowly losing control, feeling the need to put the brakes on my mind, and quickly.

"There is no right answer. Some like to say goodbye. Others like to remember loved ones as they were. It's a personal decision. We can give you time to think about it, but it's your decision. You are in control."

"He was in the car all day! What does he look like?" I was reeling. Lost. Spiraling. The first of many times when visions of that day would suddenly, grotesquely materialize in my mind. *He's lying on a bed of cold metal*, I thought. There is a blanket that will be pulled back, inside a car, all day, the sun, it had been so hot today. I could not verbalize these thoughts. I feared it would shock them. The words should die with me.

"He looks fairly normal. Just… hot," she replied.

"I need a therapist. Can I see a therapist so she can tell me, psychologically, if I will regret this?"

"We'll page her now," she said as they walked out.

I could not breathe. The room was closing in. My thoughts were evaporating like mist; they could no longer be connected but were floating further away into the night. As they left the room, curtains closed, Michele took her space of strength before me, as she would for weeks to come. Placing both hands on my shoulders, I thought she might shake me. I wish she had, but her hands remained firm and still.

"Look at me. Look at me," she stated. "You are in control. Everything you do from here on out is your decision alone. You. Are. In. Control. Okay? It's your decision."

The crisis counselor walked in and brought with her a physical calm. She spoke of trauma, religion, personal decisions of how to let go of that which was once part of you. "But either way, you have to be comfortable with your decision. You have time."

I looked at her and Michele. "I can't. I can't. I want to remember him like he was this weekend. He was so happy. We were all so happy. He was beautiful," I sobbed.

"That's fine," they all said. Michele hugged me.

The Connecticut State Department of Children and Families (DCF) petition would later state that both parents were offered a chance to see their son. Both refused. I could not know this yet, the part where there was a right and wrong, not a personal, of how to remember a child and say goodbye, to let go of that which is part of you, therefore impossible.

With her words, the waves of shock gently caressed my body, washing away any residue of my rational mind. My muscles began quivering uncontrollably, legs balking at the weight of my body. The nausea came in cycles. My lips could not convert thoughts into words, in form or in order.

"I don't... know... cold.... I'm shivering." My teeth chattered as I spoke.

"You need to lie down," Michele and the counselor said in unison.

"Grab a blanket," I heard someone say.

"Maybe shock," I responded as I lay back, feeling only the gentle rhythm of thoughts flow in and out of my mind, ever so slowly lulling me into a daze.

10

Spring 2004

I had seen his blue eyes once before. It was on the psychiatric ward at the University of North Carolina Hospital in Chapel Hill, North Carolina. We had called her "Crazy Mary." At first, we thought ourselves to be normal, and certain others were crazy. We took solace in that division in ranks. She towered above us all, fifty, if I had to guess, with a slight slump of the shoulders. (*From bearing a lifetime of burdens?* I wondered.) She wore ragged clothes and had long, stringy gray hair. She talked to herself. We stayed away, since we were normal. If we got too close, she would break in two, and we would have to stand back, gawking, as the nurses dragged her away to solitary confinement.

    I saw her months later, matted hair hanging down over her face, legs pulled up to her chest while she sat on the sidewalk on Main Street in our small university town, as we who were normal walked by. I was taking post-graduate courses to apply to medical school and briskly walking to study at a coffee shop. Years of studying in undergraduate to enable me to apply to law school had morphed into a desire to pursue something more meaningful to me, where I could use my struggles to help others in the field of psychiatry. (I would ultimately fail in this pursuit due to the limitations presented by my mental illness, resorting to becoming a lawyer in the end, but I was determined to try.) I was stable for the moment, but she was not. When she glanced up to grab the sandwich I offered her, those same blue eyes stared back at me. She did not recognize me, for her mind had fallen into a state of psychosis. She was only a shell of herself. A *thank you* but nothing clicking in her brain, though for some reason, I wanted her to remember me. I lingered for an additional moment, needing time to explore her eyes, which spoke:

I am you,
and you are me,
there is nothing
solitary
about us,
and quite possibly,
that
is the unspeakable
of sky blue,
oceans of pain,
merging
into one.

11

Summer 1999

I stood waist deep in water, cotton dress floating on the surface around me like an umbrella, eyes of the congregation upon me, staring. *I have accepted Jesus into my heart.* The preacher supported my head. *He died for my sins.* He gently pulled me backward. *He is my salvation.* Frigid water washed over my body. My soul was being washed clean. He briskly raised me up, presenting the new me, and the congregation clapped, some shouting, "Amen!" I coughed up water as I looked at their faces, but I was finally free.

I was twenty when I was baptized. "I want to wait until I feel something," I had told my parents, "not do it just because it is expected." I had been raised to believe in a God much like me. I was made in his image; he had human feelings and experiences, guided the events of history, saved and punished. Yet a distance sat between me and Him. He was out there, and I was in here, a gulf between—which I could not cross on my own. Only Jesus could save me, bring me back to God, to Heaven. Only the Word of God.

The Word failed me the night Ben died. It was not enough. I had been taught, if this moment ever came, breaths would flow from my faith in God and Heaven, but when the moment actually became, there were no words that could save me. Instead, in the instant after the calm, I had drawn a stifled gasp, thinking that this was punishment for my sins, for my human imperfections. That it was meant to teach me something, to bring me back to God, for I had fallen. I only found myself confused, lost. *No one deserves this, no matter their failures*, I thought. So who was this God that I had grown to know and trust?

I had become a Christian through my parents, yet, when Michele asked if they should be called to be with me, I faltered. "Keep them in a separate room," I had told her. I could not bear to hear their words, see their wet eyes, for it was their God—of the righteous, which I was not—who had done this to punish me. I feared they would pray and question, and in that moment, I felt no God to whom to pray. I needed only one thing—for them to be strong and pretend, still, that everything was going to be alright.

I saw our pastor first. He was tall, lanky, and had dark hair tinged with flecks of gray. He seemed out of place, not wearing his pulpit robe, instead only khakis and a plaid shirt. He appeared mortal, something I had never considered. When he walked into the room, I sensed there were no lessons that could have prepared him, no words that could have filled the void or touched the pain he witnessed.

"Did they tell you?" I asked.

"Generally, yes, they did."

"Because I can't say it yet."

He nodded his head in understanding. Words escaped us. We stood in silence, a stuttering of sorts, tears and sorrow. "Shall we pray?" he asked, since he felt he could do nothing else to quell the pain. We all held hands while he prayed to the God that was, of Ben. I heard no words, feeling only the vibration of his voice, as light and sound merged into darkness.

Afterward, I finally relented, and the nurse led me back to the small receiving room to face once more a cast of people, now including my parents and pastor. I felt like I was being presented to an audience, my final farewell. As the door closed behind me, I immediately instructed my parents, "I can't handle crying. Just please don't cry."

"We won't," they replied, gulping back the tears. "We love you." I knew they were in shock too. I held my breath once more, as if to keep the words *he is dead* from escaping, if just for one moment longer. The pastor held his hands out to us, and with eyes closed, sound and light merged into the darkness once more.

12

After a few hours, everyone finally left, concluding that my husband and I could be alone together, save one custodial night guard to watch over us. We had both been sedated, and I ventured from my room one last time before succumbing to the hollow call of deep slumber. The silence of the night bore holes through my body. Being alone with him meant I could no longer stifle the questions running rabid through my brain. Medication had blunted his primal response; his keening had ceased. He tried to make conversations, to hold me, so we could grieve together, but as he held out his arms toward me, I slipped to the end of the bed, glaring at him.

"I can't touch you or even look at you right now until you tell me the truth. What were you thinking about when you drove out of our driveway? How could you forget him? He was our son! If you simply forgot, I can forgive you. I just need to know you weren't frustrated and forgot him. Just explain it to me! How can this happen?" My voice escalated with each word.

"No, when I drove out of the driveway, I'd forgotten everything. I wasn't thinking about anything, just driving."

"I don't believe you; I heard the rocks fly as you pulled away. You were flustered from our entire hectic morning!"

It had been an ordinary day for a family of five, and busy. My parents were visiting for the Fourth of July weekend, bringing their dog with them. The morning had been bustling with extra bodies and more sounds.

Silence filled the gulf between us.

"You get that, right? You left Ben in the car all day! He was left *alone*. You forgot him, and he died! I can't hold him anymore, and I had no say in this!"

I hit the bed with my fist, a less than satisfying substitution because I wanted to hit him. Hard. I saw the night guard glance into the room.

"I've got to go."

"No," he kept repeating as I walked defiantly out of the room.

*****

Ghostly wisps of fog began to gently roll in to gather any remnants of me as I lay alone in my hospital room. I had pulled the nurse aside to tell her I was bipolar and needed to sleep. "If I don't sleep, I'm worried I may start to cycle and won't be able to keep our life together," I explained. I had to be strong for them. They called an Ativan in for me, and it had begun to work. I had drawn the curtains, lights dimmed, so I could be released completely into the mouth of darkness. I could not bear to be near Kyle, not that night. I could imagine the comfort of lying in his arms, grieving as husband and wife, but in that moment, there was too much anger and shock for me to give in. If I gave in, he would think he was forgiven.

"You don't look anywhere near sleep," the therapist stated, making one last visit to my room. "Do you need more medication?"

"Yes."

As the next dose began to ease the pounding of my mind, I felt as if sleep had anchored just offshore. The fog finally came in, drawing its heavy, sensual fingers around my mind, capturing the deep blue of the sky in his blue eyes, then falling as a curtain, and as it drew my mind out to sea, the waves lapped a sullen lullaby of *Mama, Mama* into the night.

13

I slept within a dreamless sea of fluorescence, tossing and turning, scraping the metal rails of the bed. A dissonance spread through my brain, even in sleep. My body sensed something had gone drastically wrong in the outside world. The new reality that met my eyes upon waking was stark and deafening. I craved the ability to shut my eyes again and return to the void of darkness the night had brought.

My mind groaned and wallowed its way out of the mire as I tumbled out of bed. I felt nothing but the cold tiles beneath my feet and the urge to leave, run far away from here, where my husband lay catatonic in the room next door, where my son lay dead, alone, forever. I reached instinctively for my phone, begging my parents to come take us home immediately.

A line of doctors and therapists rushed back and forth between our rooms, as if to form a bridge of sorts between two estranged lovers. The therapist, exhausted and weak, looked aged from the night.

"These are the grief counselors we recommend. Please call them," she informed me, handing me papers. "You have a psychiatrist. Correct? Here are the names of other therapists for you too."

I felt as if I were walking away equipped with a survival packet, but one with only blank pages. My fingers grasped the papers, but my mind could not yet grasp their content. Outside the door, I noticed Kyle shuffling down the hallway, a nurse holding his elbow. I pulled the curtains back to get a better look. His face held only a blank stare, showing no emotion. Not pain. Not grief. He had awoken as a zombie.

My parents arrived quickly, waiting outside for me as I had asked. I found myself nearly running through the hallway toward the exit sign, gasping for a breath of fresh air. I crashed through the sliding glass doors onto the walkway, hands covering my face, rushing toward where they stood several feet away. I walked past them, avoiding their outstretched arms. "Don't touch me," I said, pacing up and down the walkway, cars driving by with gawking faces plastered to the windows. I ran my hands through disheveled hair, at times attempting to pull out some of the more delicate strands. They relented, weak, like me. I was finally able to scream and howl the words that I had kept down the night before. They stood watching as tears ran down their faces.

"Ben's dead!

"Kyle forgot him. He laid there screaming and screaming for me and I didn't know and he sweated and burned... to... death. *Alone*!"

No amount of screaming could expunge my pain and disbelief. Unlike the night before, I had garnered the power to attempt translation myself. Hearing the words could possibly allow my brain to believe the impossible.

"We've got to leave. Let's go," I said as I turned, sobbing, seeing their hands reaching for me again. In an instant, I rushed back inside the hospital to gather my belongings.

Moments later as we drove away, I noticed my nerves were raw to the world, as if no skin protected them from the slightest sensation. The brightness of sunlight piercing through the windshield, the torrid July heat, bumps in the road which now elicited a startle response. I jumped and shook as we careened toward the unknown. My legs stuck to the leather seats, and in my periphery, I noticed Kyle sitting slumped and motionless. The living dead. And for a moment I was glad. The space between us grew. My body convulsed. Being near him was unbearable.

"Take me straight to the police station. Now," I told my father as we sped toward home.

14

November 2001

Touch is metaphysical, uniting the most organic movement of skin against skin, blood pulsing, nerves firing, of real life, with the invisible universal realm of gravity, of me falling into you, of you catching me. As a young adult, I had recoiled from touch, as I was too independent, until the day it was unavoidable.

"Let's do it, now. Not next spring, or next month, but as soon as possible. I just want to love you," I told him.

There was an urgency in my pleading, an urgency in our need to fall into someone or something beyond the structure of the world around us, which had just dramatically tumbled to ruins. To be touched, and touch another. *I need to know there is more than this*, I had felt, and so had he, my then-boyfriend of two years. We were living together at the time, wading through the last shedding of collegiate adolescence. Kyle had spent the better part of the summer gathering enough nerve to propose to me. The ring sat in his dresser drawer for months. I had tiptoed around an engagement. I was not able to let myself be pinned down, not quite yet. Law school applications needed to be finalized. I would soon be a lawyer, successful, happy. I could not allow myself to need anyone.

But we had just lived a day when the skin and bones of our world had failed. When all of it, the lights, sounds, cement, and mortar girding our reality moaned and sputtered to a grinding halt, in a deafening crash of all of us, down, into one another. It was the day I began to question the God I'd known. The stories of any one God that had been transcribed from the heavens onto paper. That had been morphed by human minds, to serve human needs, with their limitations and boundaries.

I remembered so clearly the day I had driven home from class on September 11, 2001. I heard a world of silence seeping through the speakers in the car. Static and stillness. I could not help but wonder: Was that the Word of God? The silence of a world in painful love.

I accepted his proposal two months later. "Life's too short," I'd said. *There is something… coming or going, rising or falling. I just don't know yet, but there is more than this,* I thought. It was mid-November when we found ourselves sitting together in the car at a shopping center parking lot in Raleigh, North Carolina.

"I don't want to wait," I'd drawn from the air.

"What do you mean?" he inquired.

"Let's just get married now, as soon as possible. We just have to get our marriage certificate."

"Just us?"

"Yes, just us."

Two weeks later, we stood at our local county clerk's office, him wearing khakis and me wearing black pants. No suit, no dress, just us standing in a new world, where there just may not be enough time left, where a definite life and death existed, and the expanse between which we were now forced to navigate.

"Do you have witnesses?" the clerk asked.

"No, sorry," we stuttered in unison. Embarrassed.

"Please stand to the side and try to find witnesses."

We looked around, finally arranging for two strangers, a man and woman, to witness our union.

When the ceremony was complete, we walked off into the night holding hands. Longing, searching, to be touched and to touch one another, not just in the physical sense but in another way, which we could not yet understand. I felt the energy of his hand intertwined with mine, beneath the moonlight and stars, which seemed to hide a universe of secrets just beyond our reach.

Later that night, as he touched me, I did not question the meaning of the words he had spoken. "I do. Love you, forever, and all of you." I did not need to know if his words would reach to the all of me that would exist one day. I only needed the present. The fleeting present. Quite possibly there had been an uneasiness even that night, a quiet shying away from his touch and his love. It was a gentle fear, beneath the undulations of moonlight seeping in through the shades. A fear that his words would fall apart, one day, when he would see all of me.

When I sat with him on the couch and first announced my sense of something being wrong, I needed him to still mean what he had said. The "I do, love all of you." And he did. Neither of us could translate the signs slowly growing inside of my body and mind, an uneasiness and agitation with sharp, dark edges.

I love you. I need you. Please help me.

"I will love all of you, always," he said as he hugged me tightly.

Years later, as I lay in bed with him, tracing the lines of his muscular shoulders with my fingers, I would think back to our first night together. He had no forewarning of what it would mean to love me. What it would mean to be responsible for keeping someone alive. That I would one day throw things in a mixed state, tell him I hated him, and try to leave him. He could not have envisioned his twenty-two-year-old self one day having to simply say, "No, you are not allowed to leave me. You are not allowed to die."

15

A female police officer was sitting behind bullet proof glass as I entered the police station. "I want to see a detective—now," I told her without taking a breath. My home had been a crime scene the night before, with no entry allowed. I needed to know what my home was now. An officer guided me to the same conference room where I had been taken the day prior. Mahogany conference table, plaques lining the brown, paneled walls. I scanned the room looking for video cameras.

"Mrs. Seitz," a man said apologetically as he entered the room, introducing himself as the lead detective. He was only a few inches taller than me, stout, with a tempered face. "Please have a seat," he prodded me.

"No, I'll stand."

His eyes responded with pity, sorrow, disbelief, and something else I could not discern as I tried to read him.

He reached for my hand. "First, I need to give you my condolences for this horrible tragedy. I can't imagine what your family is going through right now."

"Thank you." I jerked my hand away without thinking.

"I need to know what's going on right now. I have a right to know. Why are police at my house? Why is it a crime scene?" My voice was escalating. The simple act of speaking, which I had been largely unable to do the night prior, released a terror of emotions.

"We just have to do our job. You know we have administrative things to do to close the book on this."

"This was an accident! What do the police have to do with it? We're broken. We have nothing left!" My thoughts had not moved from shock back into reality yet. He was helping me put the pieces together.

"We know. We know, and we are so sorry, but we have to work with you and talk with you. It's administrative. When there is a death…"

"The media will be at our house! Do you have to release the name? Everyone will know. I have a right to privacy. This is my family; I've got to protect them!"

"Ma'am, I can delay it and try to keep it off the blotter, but you know how things get out unexpectedly."

"Your *job* is to protect us. We are citizens of this town. We'll have to move, sell our house. Our lives are over!" Sobs battered the walls as he tried to assuage my sorrow and grief.

"Ma'am, I know. We will protect you. Don't get ahead of yourself. It will be okay."

I drew my senses in for the moment. "Well, can I get access to my own house now?"

"Yes, my officers should be finishing up. Go on over," I heard him speak as I walked out the door into my new reality, headed home.

16

My reality is a nightmare, and I will awaken soon, I thought. While our children played peacefully at a friend's house, I was determined to return and reclaim our home. Rocks cracked beneath our tires as we pulled down the gravel road to our house. The green canopy of poplars and maples created a tunnel for us, and I was sure I would emerge on the other end in a world where there was still a Ben. Waiting for me. Yet when we pulled into our driveway, I saw only two police cars and an old tan house, paint cracking at the edges. *This cannot be real,* I thought, and I only wanted to turn around and escape, back down the road, back in time, to our real house with no police cars and Ben sleeping inside.

There were introductions and handshakes, a formality, as an officer asked if he could take pictures of our house. I followed the group around, dazed, not able to bear entering Ben's room. "I can't go in," I'd told them as I stood in the hallway, listening to the clicking of his camera. It was a monotonous ticking off of the moments of the day. The pictures were proof of this all being real. I followed him through the house. Click, a picture of our staircase. Click, our bedroom.

"Do you need a picture of the kitchen?" I heard a voice ask.

"No, everything looks clean and organized in here. It's fine."

"Our kitchen?" I questioned him, still in a foggy haze of unreality.

"Mrs. Seitz, we need to look at his computer. Can you open the computer and let us glance through it?"

"No, why? That's our personal property and information. A computer has nothing to do with the accident."

"Ma'am, it's just something we need to do, just to make sure."

"Make sure of what?" my voice escalated. "No, you can get a warrant if you want our computer." I was not aware at the time that several weeks prior, another father in Georgia had left his son in a hot car, and evidence had been found in his computer's search history.

"Yes, I can get a warrant, but it may be easiest if you just let us glance through," he stated, calmly. "Then we can be done and get out of your hair."

I relented. *I just need this to be over*, I thought. *I'm a lawyer. I understand.* I opened our blue laptop and typed in our password.

"Is this your only family computer?" he asked.

"Yes. So, what do you want to see?" I inquired.

"What browser does he use? Can you just scroll through the history?" he asked.

Pulling up Google Chrome, I finally found the history page and scrolled through a month of browsing history, droning out loud as I scrolled: "ESPN, Neymar, soccer games, ESPN again, Patriots, SCOR, that's our soccer league by the way, how to grow a garden, ESPN." I looked at him. "So, my husband likes sports. Did you get what you needed? Anything else?"

He smiled, sensing my sarcasm. "No, ma'am, that's good. Thank you."

Shutting the computer, I stood to walk back into the kitchen.

"One last thing," asked the detective. "We have your husband's phone but it is password protected. Can you give me his password?"

"No. This is it. If you want access to his phone, get a warrant," I responded.

"Oh, I will. We're working on it right now," he stated.

"Good, you do that. Come back when it's ready." I ushered them out, closing the door behind them. As I watched their cars back out of the driveway, I was transfixed and stood unmoving by our front window. *Just breathe*, I had to remind myself.

17

The wood beneath my fingers as I pulled myself up the stairs. *This is real*, I thought. The nursery to the left, where I could not allow my eyes to shift. *That is real.* Our bedroom and once peaceful sleep, baby monitor crackling as Ben babbled in his crib, shifting, alive. *That was real, and this cannot be.* I was in a dream within a dream, searching to find my way out as I climbed the stairs to our bedroom. I had to pack everything. I did not know when we would be able to return to our house, if ever. We were in hiding. My mother walked a distance behind, wary, unsure.

I entered the bedroom where there had once been breathing and laughter, but which was now only an empty reservoir of our lives. His pajamas, white with an alligator near the hem, green around the shoulders, lay crumpled on the bed where Kyle had changed him the day before. Still fresh from a lazy boy's night's sleep, seemingly waiting to be worn again. There would not be a Ben, to come home, to slip them on. I retched the fragments of my life and fell onto the bed, burying his pajamas into my body.

With a gasp of sorrow, I grabbed the pajamas and rammed them against my nose as I inhaled his scent.

"Oh my god! I can still smell him! I don't understand. I can smell him!" I screamed toward my mother as she walked hesitantly closer, choking back tears.

"What do I do? I need to keep his smell. I can't lose it! It's all I have left!" Shaking, a screaming wail of grief and shock.

"Honey," she stopped walking.

"If I put them in a Ziploc bag, they'll start to smell like plastic! So what do I do, physically, to keep the smell?"

"You should just let them be for now," she stated.

Grief quickly turned to fury as I raced out of the bedroom and through the house, still holding his pajamas to my nose, tears merging with the remaining atoms of him. Visions popped in and out of my head. Kyle was holding him yesterday morning in our bathroom. He wore these wrinkled pajamas.

"This is all I have left," I howled, trying to lay my eyes on everything else around the house that was Ben. Books strewn in the living room, basketball hoop in the sunroom, balls lying silent and forlorn, bouncy house in the dining room.

I made my way down our hallway until my parents stopped me. With no physical outlet for my pain, I could only scream.

"I hate him." My body shook with the words. "My son is dead and I don't get him back. I just want to let them hang him out to dry. The police, let them have him."

I saw a tear trembling on my mother's cheek, and as she drew me closer, I collapsed into her shoulder with stifled sobs. In this dream within a dream, the only truth I knew was that the pajamas I held in my hands were real. They would not be worn again, and now there was only a space where he once was and a visceral need of a mother to hold him again. As I untangled my body from the web of her arms, I felt only a pain beyond sensation. A slow disgorging of all of me. I expected to see the pieces of me tumble out onto our hardwood floors, but as I looked down, I found nothing but skin and bones, muscles of hands pulled taut. I was still holding tightly to his alligator pajamas. A silent suffocation.

18

Summer 1989

I had known death before. I was ten, and she was more than a grandmother. In the ways of youth, I felt as if she were an angel, for when she stood beside me, she wasn't inches away. She was inside of me, part of me, before and after, and forever. I called it love at the time. I knew nothing more, nothing less. It was the love of a child and her mother, once removed.

I still remember her standing before me, sturdy and tall, white coiffed hair, inside her country farmhouse in rural South Carolina. The white refrigerator outlined her body. My mind took a photograph of that instant, to keep.

"Lordy mercy my back hurts, sweetie." Her words dripped like honey.

"I'm sorry, Mama Ruthie." I gave her a hug. Her pain was my pain.

"I'm sure it's just a pinched nerve, honey." As she hobbled away to finish cooking, the smell of cornbread and fresh collard greens permeated the air.

Months later, I was placed on cushioned metal chairs, off to the right of the photograph on the covered patio. My parents as bookends. "Mama Ruthie has cancer," they told me.

"What kind?" I inquired.

"It's multiple myeloma, baby, in her bones, but we are treating it."

I knew cancer and I knew death, and I had heard them used together quite often.

"Will she die?" I asked.

"We don't think so, not right now," they responded, touching my hair.

However, a year later, she would indeed die, in an intensive care unit while I was sleeping, and I would sift through the running reel of photographs from that day. I had sat on the patio staring out the window at our farm, an ancient black walnut tree with a rope swing hanging from its branches. Tears speckled my cheeks, tan from the summer sun, as I had run through the garden onto the hilly fields, down, falling farther, farther down, to the creek that flowed through our property. The touch of dry, green and yellow grass against my shins, the smell of animals mixing with sweet Southern heat, the sound of wind, birds perched in trees, a babbling creek in the distance.

But I love her, I thought as I ran, my lips trembling, choking back tears. *I don't understand that part. The part where she is here but may not be one day.* The feel of her soft skin against my back, lying in bed with her. "Tickle me, Mama Ruthie," I would whisper to feel the touch of her. Or sitting beside her at our white antique piano in the parlor, which held the smell of an aged reverence. "Sing to me, Mama Ruthie," I would squeal with glee to hear the sound of her. I listened in silent wonder.

"Yes, we'll gather at the river, the beautiful, the beautiful river…" Her voice was liquid, carrying the deep tones. That was real, so what was this thing called death?

Between the time of living and dying, she had sat at that same river, playing cowboys and Indians with me as I ran through the river bed, chanting with a pretend feather in my hair. She allowed me to continue in my innocence. *Just a bit more,* I'm sure she had thought.

"It's hard for me to get up, sweetie. Can you give me a hand?" she asked with a grunt, and with her grunt, I felt a pain of sorts. Yet it was also a love and longing. But for what? Another day, another reality where there was a babbling creek and a grandmother with no cancer?

And time, so much more time? In that instant of youth, though, I felt a longing to hang on to the moment, when it was just us alone, playing among the riverbed, birds calling above, and laughter. I yearned to stop time, to hold it close to me and never let go.

*****

"You can't take all this with you when you die!" The preacher shook his hands wildly, causing the congregation to look around the sanctuary. She had passed away months ago, and we were all finding our footing this Sunday morning, in the little brick church a mile from the farm.

"The cars. The money. The houses. None of it."

We waited for the rest. What we could take with us. My feet could not even touch the floor. They dangled like a rag doll. Black patent shoes, white laced socks turned down, flowered dress, buttoned up high, curls streaming down my back, blue bow set on top.

"We are all sinners, fallen angels. But you *can* inherit the kingdom of God. Do you want to know how?"

I shook my head, looking around the country sanctuary as older women fanned themselves with the morning's bulletin, hands in the air, fervently mumbling, "Yes!"

"You accept Jesus Christ into your heart as your savior," he stated, then paused, "and you *will* inherit the kingdom of God."

The organ began to play as he asked us to close our eyes while the newly saved walked up to the pulpit.

I envisioned this God, a man like us, sitting on a throne with Jesus at his feet, angels with white wings and clouds. I thought about the rules I had to follow and the hell and brimstone I feared. It was more than simply accepting Jesus into my heart. It was also avoiding the need for forgiveness. What if He can't forgive me if I sin? What if my sin is too great? I was scared. What about everyone else who isn't sitting in a church right now learning this? They will all go to hell. I saw flames and a devil with a pitchfork, grinning with sinister satisfaction. I needed to find salvation, but I didn't feel anything yet, and that worried me.

As I skipped down the front stairs of the church, arms swung on each side by my mother and father, grandfather following a step behind, head hung in supplication, I decided to wait to figure it all out. The *why*, I really just loved to jump up and down and feel the summer breeze ruffle my dress, listen to the fizz of a Pepsi in my throat from the country store next door, taste the Moon Pies. The *what* was really there after this all fell away. There would be time for that. In that moment, I just wanted to live.

19

As we sped away, the memories consumed me. The driveway where Kaylyn had ridden her bicycle for the first time, screaming with glee, then rushing inside with a bloodied knee. I healed it with a gentle kiss and a bandage. The leaves would be turning in fall, deep orange and red. We had raked piles right there. In that spot to the right of the white oak, beneath the swing. They had run and jumped, disappearing only to reappear with laughter and hair matted with leaves. The canopy of trees above the gravel road had hung down, as if in prayer the year before, weighty with the winter's first snow.

Now all surreal, dropping off a cliff into history. Gone. Swallowed whole. I turned to the future, anxiety rising as the moments passed in my mind. Visions, fulsome with possibility. We pack boxes. We leave. Kyle walks into the police station, silver handcuffs glistening in the sun. Television segments, news articles, whispers, and judgment. "She has a mental illness, you know," I hear them say. Everyone knows. I lose my life too.

My muscles quivered as the angst rose, too strong even for tears to escape. The dream within a dream began to slip away into a void within me. The green New England canopy rose above us as we raced down the gravel path. Rays of sunlight speckled the hood of our car. Time appeared frozen, and in a singular moment, a peace overcame me. The fear slipped away and instead a vision of Ben, sandy blond hair reflecting the sun, arose in my mind. A sense of bliss enveloped me.

I had been taught that Heaven was high above and that Ben was there, far out of reach, far from me and the physical world. He could not touch me anymore. If that were true, why did the peace that had just overcome me feel so intimately like Ben and the soft caress of his hands against my chest as I had rocked him off to sleep? "It's okay, Mommy. It will all be okay," he seemed to speak as his eyes finally closed into a world of dreams.

20

Fall 2002

Running from life, from myself, was not new to me. It was habitual and comfortable. I had found myself sitting behind a steering wheel before. Just driving. To nowhere, to anywhere but where I was. The first time had been instinctive, thoughtless. I landed in an empty parking lot in Durham, North Carolina. It had happened in a blur, and I had forgotten how I had even arrived there.

The rain pounded the windshield as I heard my phone buzz and answered instinctively. I wasn't sure I wanted to be found, or talk to anyone for that matter, but a human voice could talk me down, and I was sure it was my psychiatrist.

"Hello?" I answered automatically.

"Lindsey, where are you?" she asked, halfway believing she would get an answer.

Minutes passed as I contemplated my options. Drive to the hospital, where I would be admitted once again and offered a new cocktail of drugs. Head to a hotel or dead end to use the medication I carried in my purse. Or return home, where I could hope to find some solace and a husband waiting to welcome me.

Like most other times I had found myself behind the wheel just driving, I did not want to hurt myself. I only wanted to be somewhere, other than here, with a mind spiraling out of control, waiting for someone to help. What I did not know at the time and would learn after Ben's death was that no one could help me. I would have to help myself.

After what seemed like thirty minutes of back and forth, we made hasty plans that I would return home and try to sleep off the agitation. I would see her Monday and we would make a new game plan together.

I often look back to those endless days and nights of driving aimlessly around the back roads of North Carolina and realize they represented something symptomatic of my illness and of society. I, like many others, could not settle into my own skin. I could not accept myself or others' help at that time. I could only run. I would continue running for years, hiding in the shadows, waiting until the moment came when I could first accept myself before I ever asked others to understand me.

What is it about mental illness that cloaks so many in secrecy? It is the unspeakable. We live without a voice out of fear. It is a fear born out of societal stigma. Fear of losing jobs, losing friends, facing whispers behind closed doors. So I found myself running from life itself, never feeling fulfilled as an individual because I could not be true to myself. Remaining hidden in the shadows was safe. Remaining chained yet yearning to be free.

21

We had all sat around the fire pit on Michele's back porch last fall. The sound of football announcers blaring in the background, the crack of helmets and play calls. As the sky grew darker, we called the kids up from the basement and unpacked the graham crackers, chocolate, and marshmallows for s'mores. Ben sat peacefully in his bouncy seat beside us, sucking his pacifier vigorously with a smile on his face and watching the action. He was content. He was with us. When he tired, Kyle rocked him in the back bedroom before placing him gently in the pack-n-play for a nap. It was the same bedroom where Kyle now lay nearly catatonic. I was not sure I could handle the onslaught of memories, but it was the only place we could be. It was Ben's second home, and it would now be our safe haven.

Michele's husband, Chris, met us at the top of the stairs when we arrived. His hug engulfed me as he choked back tears. "I'm so sorry." He looked at me and then away again. "It's hard to see him like this." He guided me to the bedroom where Kyle lay staring into the void of our life. I sat on the edge of the bed, allowing his arms to instinctively draw me closer as I shuddered internally, longing to escape his grasp.

"I've got all our things from the house," I explained. "We are safe for now."

"I'm so sorry." His body shook with sobs as he held me tighter, inciting within me an instinct to pull away.

"I love you, but Ben is dead. Okay? I'm alright for now and trying to see about things. Please just rest and I'll be in the other room. Someone will always be here with you."

"Please don't leave," he cried, reaching for me.

"I've got to go see about things," I reminded him. "I'll be back; I promise."

As I walked out of the room, I turned back. "Hun, I've got to tell the kids," I said as I continued down the hallway, wretched sobs echoing behind me.

I found everyone standing in the kitchen, talking quietly. They didn't feel comfortable taking care of Kyle in his state. We needed experts, friends to rotate in and out to sit with him, a network within the community to bring food. Only friends we trusted since our address would be given out, and I agreed. I would call the grief and crisis counselors recommended by the hospital therapist. Despite my yearning to clamp down on the events that transpired, I agreed to let Michele reach out to our close friends to help take care of us, as we suspected our situation would continue to spin out of control.

Hands guided me off to the side, into the dining room, with a gentle whisper of "We need to talk." The words ushered in a rush of adrenaline. I was beginning to learn my body's trauma response, my sympathetic nervous system readying itself for fight or flight. The physical symptoms, a rush of adrenaline and racing pulse, skipped the circuits of my brain entirely. It was visceral. Anything could trigger it—a memory of Ben or the day he died, a sudden movement, a loud noise or unexpected touch, and most strongly, any inclination of a new stressor or new unknown. It began as a sinking feeling, as my blood rushed to my legs. Metal pillars slowly sinking in quicksand. The tingling of my body turned to numbness; my mind became a blank slate. I often froze, feeling both dead and alive. I could recognize it but not control it yet.

"You need to get a lawyer, Lindsey," she stated simply.

"What? Why?" My brain still could not translate events into what they appeared to the outside world, to anyone outside my immediate circle of friends and family.

"Listen, anytime the police are involved, you need a lawyer. You know that."

I decided to allow others to tap into my rational brain for the moment and lead me. I had been engaged in flight up to this point, but it was time to change course and fight. I saw her mouth moving and heard her discussing a friend's sister, an attorney, who knew someone, who knew someone else, which all became a drone of syllables and sounds, merging into senseless chatter as my mind slowly slipped away again into a state of nothingness.

22

A golden cross hung above us. The pastor arranged the chairs so the girls would be looking at it when I told them their brother was dead. I did not yet know how this would affect them. The therapist had told me they would write their own story as time progressed. Of their brother, and how he died, and why. Whether they introduced themselves as having one sibling or two. Whether he would just fall into the past because he had been so young and they had been too. I did know they would retain a mental picture of where they heard the words, and one day, far in the future, when they uncovered photographs of our family, they would remember. Christmas cards, Ben grinning in front of the tree, two sisters kissing his cheeks on each side. Kaylyn sitting in our brown leather chair, cupping her brother's head in the crook of her arm, smiling as she fed him his bottle, his eyes already drifting off to sleep. They would remember, and I needed perfection in a broken moment.

Michele had told them their brother was sick, and they had slept unflustered at her house overnight. They ran out from the sanctuary to meet me when I arrived. Kaylyn, age eight, with light brown hair to her shoulders, muscular from years of soccer, hazel eyes carrying in them a strength and maturity beyond her years. Riley, almost six, our tiny sprite, jumping with an energy she could rarely contain, dark brown eyes, soulful and questioning. *Jesse Lee Vacation Bible School* emblazoned on their bright green and yellow t-shirts, color-coordinated by grade.

"Hey Mommy! How's Ben?" they both asked as I buried my head in their shoulders. A bear hug to belie the truth of tears beneath. I needed their world to remain intact for just a moment longer.

"How was your day?" I asked, attempting a smile. "Let's walk as you tell me. I want to talk to you in the little chapel out back." I listened without hearing their drone of happy chatter.

The building was once a carriage house turned into a chapel for smaller meetings of the congregation and prayer groups. A Bible sat on a shelf at the end of the entryway. We turned left into a side room lined with folding chairs, a small makeshift pulpit at the rear. We all took our seats in a circle, as they sat wide-eyed and watching, sensing something was awry.

"Girls, I love you so much. You know that. Right?"

They nodded and mouthed, "Yes," slowly and drawn out, unsure of my intent.

"There is something I need to tell you. Yesterday, Ben got really sick. His heart stopped beating, and we had to take him to the hospital. The doctors did everything they could, but he didn't make it. Ben died." I had decided to stick to the physical death and not use descriptors that would alter the reality. I knew they would have mountains to climb in the coming months, and they needed to know how to understand and process reality. He did not pass away; we did not lose him. He physically died. His heart stopped, and he was not coming back. There would be a time and place in the weeks to come to inform the girls as to the true events of that day.

I watched them for a response to gauge whether to stop or change course, but I was met only by wide eyes, waiting for more. I continued. "Mommy and Daddy are really sad right now, and we know you will be too. That's okay. We want you to know we are here, together. We love you and need to just be with you. It's okay to be sad, but we all need to talk about our feelings. Do you understand?"

They looked at me, nodding their heads yes, silent, faces searching. For the pastor, all that remained was for us to pray. So we did. Forming a circle, heads down, eyes closed. With the "Amen," Kaylyn stood and walked beneath the cross, looking out the window, far, far away, with an almost blank stare. Her eyes seemed to fall upon something solid and real.

"Can I go play on the playground?" she asked.

"Yes, honey, whatever you want."

She ran out the door as we followed quickly behind. The pastor walked up ahead of her, guiding her toward her grandparents. I shuffled along, lagging behind. As gentle as the wind, a tiny hand locked its fingers between mine.

"Mommy, it's okay. I love Ben too. I'm sad, but it'll be okay, Mommy. I promise. I love you," Riley said.

My legs stopped moving and I fell to my knees, laying my head against her chest so I could listen to her beating heart. "I know, but I love him so much," I sobbed, my body shaking into her solid stillness. Her hand brushed the surface of my hair as we stood, mother and daughter, outside a small chapel. Perfection in a broken moment.

23

I heard the knock at the front door as I sat comforting Kyle. I was not yet aware of the involvement of the state child protective services agency, so I remained unflustered. Michele called me into the living room where I saw a stranger standing. The first sense of foreboding entered with a slight shiver up my spine.

"Hi, ma'am. My name is Jason Miller. I'm from the Connecticut Department of Children and Families." He had an athletic build and a soft, kind face. His eyes shone with a mixture of emotions, the sorrow of inquisition.

"Can we talk for a few minutes?" he asked, attempting to shake my hand as Michele led us into her living room.

"Okay. But Michele is staying in here with us," I stated promptly as she sat down beside me on the couch.

She offered him a seat across the coffee table, establishing enough distance for what was to come. Instinct told me I needed support—and a witness.

"First, I'd like to offer my sincere condolences for what happened yesterday. I can't even imagine what you are going through," he stated.

"Thank you."

"So, Mrs. Seitz, let me tell you a little bit about what we do. I'm here to investigate the incident yesterday. Your son's death and the events leading up to it. We received a referral from the hospital with an allegation of child abuse and child neglect. Since you have existing children, we need to assess the incident and the safety of everyone, including you and your children."

"What?" I responded as he nodded his head in acknowledgment. "Fine, let's talk. I want to get this over with." I knew they had to do this. A child had died under extreme circumstances. My initial instinct was that the investigation would be basic. We were good parents, and I assumed that would come to light fairly quickly. We had nothing to hide from that day. The facts were self-evident.

"My number-one priority is my girls and controlling this situation. The media, our safety. Everything." I stuck to a summary of the day, the current whereabouts of the girls, their knowledge of Ben's death. I felt angst rising as I began to move through the timeline in my mind to Kaylyn's soccer practice that afternoon and Kyle's unresponsiveness to my texts and calls. The daycare calling to inquire about Ben while I was driving home. "He was never dropped off," they said. My mind falling apart, my muscles involuntarily driving me to the police station where I collapsed in an anxiety attack. "There is a medical emergency," the police officer told me. "We need to get you to the hospital as quickly as possible." My mind was getting closer to the moment, time, and space, when everything fell away, and it began to shut down.

"So did you see your husband's car on Main Street at the coffee shop when you drove past to take the girls to Vacation Bible School?" he asked.

With that question, with the memories, my mind began to clamp shut. I turned to Michele, mouth quivering, tears forming. "He is making me talk about that day." I could not verbalize any other cause for my physical response, but the mere *talking about* that day.

"We are done here," she responded, looking at him.

After discussing the logistics of living spaces to be assessed and support systems to be contacted, we walked him back to the bedroom, as he needed to see Kyle. Jason would write in his record that Kyle sat, appearing sad and sedated, with Chris by his side.

"Keep an eye on him," he told me.

"He has an appointment with his primary care doctor tomorrow. He doesn't have a psychiatrist," I told him.

"Is there any history of mental illness?" he inquired.

"No." A definitive no. Kyle had always been the stable one, my rock. That's why I could not understand why it was him, and not me.

As we stood in the living room once more, I saw papers circulating around. I heard a chatter of "releases, assess, records, we need..." Papers appeared in my fingers, releases for medical, education, dental records. I quickly signed. *Wait,* I thought. I had to try to rein my mind back in—from the events of that day to now, standing here. I tried to ground myself in the present. *What am I really signing?* I wondered.

Mother refused to sign all requested releases, Jason would report. *It was hard to get mother to talk or do anything that has to do with toddler,* he would state.

"I need to assess your children. Can we go talk to them?"

"No," I stated adamantly. I did not want the girls to ever have to know that an agency such as DCF existed. That children were abused and neglected. That agencies had to investigate families. To be asked questions about whether we spanked or hit them and not understand why. They were innocent and felt safe in an unsafe world. They did not know pain and negativity yet, and I wanted them to remain that way.

After more prodding, I eventually agreed. It was inevitable, and I just wanted to get it done. I needed to grieve, not focus on this. My son was dead, and I felt as if that point had been forgotten already.

"But you are not to ask them about Ben's death. I'll introduce you as my friend. I'm not going to traumatize them further."

"This situation is severe, Mrs. Seitz. Here is a safety plan. Kyle cannot be around the children unsupervised," he stated, placing the white and yellow copy paper in my hand. I remember this statement as the first warning bell, my first indication of what was to come. I was shocked by the statement, that the representative of a government agency thought he needed to instruct me how to parent. How to be a mother. Govern when and where I thought fit for the girls to be reunited with their father, who they needed so deeply in a time of mourning. I had already restricted their time with him, not out of danger, but out of the trauma that could ensue from them seeing someone they loved in a state of grief and catatonia. I became further annoyed and frustrated.

I handed the paper to Michele. "I can't read and process this. I'm not in a mental state to do so." She was not me, and not a lawyer, but she was the only safeguard I had. We both assumed I had to sign the safety plan, that there were no other options. My mind was faulty, and she needed to act as my proxy.

She read through it. "Okay, what do I do?"

Jason asked her to sign it. She handed it to me, and I signed as the caregiver. The words on the page merged into a well of ink with curves and slashes.

"Here." I pushed the paper back to him. Months later, with a clear mind, I would sit at our kitchen table re-reading the pages, comprehending for the first time what I had been forced to sign.

*****

I sat beside Kaylyn at our friend's kitchen table, Riley on my lap and Jason across from us. "He's one of my friends. He needs to talk to you because of what happened to Ben," I told them. Kaylyn looked at me inquisitively, understanding more than her younger sister, knowing this was unusual. Speaking in a kind voice, he began with easy topics. Favorite subjects at school, hobbies, colors.

As he questioned them, nervous giggles flowed around the table while they glanced at each other, to me, then back to him. They were unsure why they were being asked if we spanked them, did we leave them alone, what were our favorite drinks, how did we punish them when they got in trouble.

As he left the house, I let out a sigh of relief. The interview was over, and the girls could move on. I had no idea at the time that the battle was just beginning.

24

I could hear the sound of laughter and splashing from the pool outside as I sank deeper into the couch. One of our close friends had offered to shelter us for a few nights. I could not let the girls see Kyle in his state, and neither could I, for that matter. It was a temporary separation. I needed privacy and had asked her not to tell anyone we were there, not even the neighbors or other friends. We were all waiting for our names to be released and did not know when it would happen.

She and her daughter had made dinner for us. I heard the clink of dishes and silverware; I am sure someone must have handed me a plate. Michele had joined us with her son. We needed to keep each other busy to avoid the silence that would allow our minds to replay and analyze the unfolding events. I remember only the chatter of voices and passing of food around me, as I honed in on the laughter outside. I needed to grasp hold of it. My survival depended on it.

"I need to sleep with them," I uttered matter-of-factly, interrupting an ongoing conversation. "Can we all squeeze into your bed?" I would sleep in the middle to feel their bodies around me. I could not be alone.

As I lay between my two daughters later that night, I felt the skin of their legs against mine. It was simple and comforting. A sob emerged, stifled to avoid waking everyone else in the house. It became a silent wailing. I asked them to move closer to me, until they were touching every inch of my body, and they complied.

"What's wrong, Mommy?" Riley asked, worried.

"I don't know how to live. It hurts so bad. I love Ben so much. I wasn't ready. I just don't know how to make it. It seems impossible. My heart hurts," I cried, shaking beneath their grasp, causing them to shake with me since we had become one body.

"Mom, you just function. And you breathe. And you'll live," she responded in her high-pitched voice. As her words rose and fell in the night air, my body ceased its shaking and I fell silent, in awe of the simplicity of it all.

25

I awoke the next morning, sifting through the slush of an Ativan-induced hangover. I looked in the mirror, not recognizing the face staring back at me. Curly brown hair and eyes as puffy as small pillows, face pale from lack of sleep, too thin from lack of sustenance. I knew I had to force my mind into a new gear. The grief would have to wait. Right then, in that moment, I had to plan and consider next steps. It was a comfort to ignore grief for the time being, to deny the loss and simply focus on the protection of what I had left.

I showered and shaved, since that was functioning. I ate bites of breakfast and downed a morning coffee. When I arrived back at Michele's house, I found Kyle in much the same state. I had called the number she had given me without question, a criminal lawyer. *Criminal*, I repeated the word in my head over and over again, attempting to translate it. He would need to meet with Kyle, as his client, meaning I had to break the news to him sooner than later.

Friends had been rotating in and out of grief or suicide watch, or some combination of the two, all night. They entered to sit in silence and listen, with a kind hand and words of wisdom as needed, and emerged with swollen eyes.

"What is he talking about?" I always asked.

"Just rambling and crying. Intense grief. Worrying about you and the girls. He says you could never forgive him. That he doesn't deserve it anyway. He is worried about losing you all too," they answered.

I entered the room during Chris's rotation. "Hey hun, I love you." I kissed him on the cheek. "I need to tell you something, though," I stated, sitting beside him on the bed.

"Huh?" he asked, his mind still a slushy mixture of pain and shock.

"We need to get a lawyer. I have one coming over today. Michele's friend recommended him, and I have colleagues from work asking around to confirm he is the right person. He will need to at least see you today. Okay?"

"What?" A blank expression. "A lawyer? Why?"

"Well, the police are involved. He's a criminal attorney," I informed him. *Just stick to the facts*, I reminded myself.

"Let them. Let them do whatever they want to me. They can't hurt me. They can't punish me any more than I am punishing myself!" he wailed, veins throbbing, sweat beginning to roll down his face.

"I know. Listen, don't worry about this part of it. This is why I'm an attorney. I'll take care of everything. Okay? You have to trust me."

He only stared as I gave him a hug and walked away.

*****

John Robert Gulash, who we would later just call Bob, arrived in the afternoon, wearing a gray suit and carrying a briefcase. He looked authoritative, which I desperately needed. I had spent the day sifting through, organizing, and prioritizing the pieces of our life, which I now carried like puzzle pieces in a burlap bag thrown precariously over my shoulder, to one day reassemble. I felt as if I was navigating a barren desert with land mines hidden below the surface, cracked and thirsty. I craved the cool drink of another's knowledge and strength, someone who could take one piece out of the bag, lightening the load.

We sat on the deck, and he offered his condolences. As he leaned forward to look into my eyes (an act so many others avoided), I examined the details of the authority he was offering. The gray-tinged hair, tiny crow's feet from years of strenuous reading, arguing, and comforting clients. He straightened his tie.

"You'll learn this about me, Lindsey. I always expect the worst. I just have too much experience with prosecutors. I hope they don't, but I am sure they will charge him with something."

Okay, okay.

Charges, homicide, negligence.

Jail, probation.

Just please carry this piece for me, I thought as I sat listening. We would be running again soon, but for this single moment in time, I needed to sit and allow the burdens to be lifted into the scorching hot summer sky. I had to believe... that he could save us.

26

"Oh my God!"

Chills ran up my spine as a rush of adrenaline pulsated through my chest. I knew immediately—with the words, the enunciation, the suddenness of the exclamation—that my sense of control over my life was coming to a grinding halt.

"What?" I yelped, equaling her urgency.

"Lindsey, they've announced the names at the press conference. Ben's and Kyle's."

"Our names?" I felt myself silently hyperventilating and began pacing.

"It's everywhere, already on Facebook and in the news."

We both stood staring, allowing our minds to catch up to the spinning world. As I paced, the cadence of my thoughts began to match my steps and frantic breathing.

"Okay. I've got to take down our Facebook pages. We've got to go somewhere else. People know we are at your house. We've got to leave."

"Right, how about Jen's house?"

We needed to turn the nonsensical world into logical steps for humans to follow.

"Oh my god, my parents are at our house. Where's my phone?" I fumbled over the countertop until I found it and dialed.

When my mother answered, I said, "Mom, I can't explain more. There's no time. They announced our names at a press conference.

You have twenty minutes at most to pack everything and get out of our house before the media arrives. Do it now! Please, please do it. I know you want to stay to protect the house, but don't argue. Just trust me. You have no idea what's about to happen." I had watched the news enough each summer to know the media frenzy accompanying hot car deaths.

As she turned out of our private gravel driveway twenty minutes later, a white media van was quickly approaching.

27

Riley sat on Kyle's lap looking forlorn, one leg nervously tapping the coffee table in front of her. Her eyes never looked up. She, being overly sensitive, could not gather her thoughts into words, as I am sure she sensed something was very wrong with her father. Kaylyn sat to his right, jabbering. She had taken on her role as the talker to fill the space of silence where Ben used to be. She discussed her day, anything other than why we were all there, sitting in Michele's living room, allowing a father to be reintroduced to his children. He sat with a drug-induced blank stare, alternating from gazing at an empty space across the room to watching her mouth move. Expressionless, he feigned attention.

It was Wednesday night and they had begged to see him. We obliged, not wanting to insinuate that something was drastically wrong. We would be moving as a family the next morning to stay in another friend's house while she was on vacation. We would have privacy, which we so desperately needed, and a base camp for grief and planning. Jason had approved the dwelling with the condition that Kyle sleep separately in the in-law suite.

As we settled in the next morning, we knew we would have two days to prepare for the memorial service and were falling behind. We were shadows moving in a dreamlike state, not realistically functional quite yet. The house became a center point for all activity, with the bustle of hugs and chatter inside rooms, food being received and served, a constant dinging of my phone with messages from family and friends as news began to trickle out of who we were and what had happened. The girls' friends were hustled in and out to keep them happy and laughing. We hoped the pure taste of ice cream and time warp of a soccer game could distract them from the prospects of death.

A vision had begun to pop into my head. I stood above a white casket that sat in a hole in the ground. I shoveled dirt on top. It turned into a mound. Dust to dust. Dirt, earth, body. I had business to attend to that Thursday. Planning the funeral.

28

We sat together at the patio table, the pastor beside Kyle (who never took his gaze away from the table's surface). It was a scorching summer day. We squinted to see each other, sweat rapidly forming on our faces. A slow torture of memories. I needed something from our pastor that he would never be able to give me. I yearned for it. I felt as if I would die without it. I needed comfort. I was not certain whether I still believed in God, or at least one that would punish me for my sins by taking my son. Quite possibly I had begun to transition to a state of apathy, which I feared was the precursor to a silent surrender.

It's fine if humans simply created stories of a God to help them make sense of life, I thought, *to comfort them through hardships, help explain suffering. Life and death.* As I looked at him, I only needed him to make me feel better, comfort me, lie to me if he had to. I was setting him up for failure from the start. It was an impossible request. The umbrella shaded part of his face. I wondered if he was nervous.

"I need to know Heaven is real. I need to know where Ben is," I proclaimed, because he was not here. He was gone and Saturday he would be in the ground beneath a mound of dirt. The vision of broken ground darted through my brain once more. "Will I see him again? I wasn't ready to say goodbye. If there is a Heaven, will I recognize him?" The pastor could not save me half-heartedly. He could not save me with just Heaven; it had to be a Heaven where I would recognize my son.

He leaned into the shade to look into my eyes. "Yes, Heaven is real," he said, "and I believe you will recognize him." He quoted some Bible verses.

Beads of sweat slid down our faces. I watched the heat pulsate around me. I shifted uncomfortably in my seat.

"But you don't know for sure." That was my only truth as we sat there planning a funeral, Kyle catatonic. I did not want faith or belief anymore. I needed to *know* I would see Ben again, or I would not make it through. I needed certainty. I had completely skipped over the question of whether there was a God, for I was not sure I could believe in a God who would do this or stand by and allow this to occur.

So I didn't really want to know.

In that moment.

If God was real.

No words could help, so I changed gears. We needed to plan. I could control by planning. We discussed the need for a private burial. The afternoon before the service. The media would not expect that. I found a slight sense of accomplishment in outsmarting the media. It was a little something, a slight lifting of my spirits. I saw a vision of a crowd in the distance, wearing black, gathered around a small white casket, tombstones, and a news caption beneath. I could not allow that invasion of our need to grieve.

"What songs do you want?" he asked, taking notes. "Who do you want to speak? To give the eulogy? Do you want to receive friends? Do you want a picture of him displayed?"

My mind started to spin again. Only phrases and visions. Funeral, eulogy, son, blue eyes, cheesy grin, in the ground. I must have been speaking in choppy phrases.

"I'll give you some time to think about it, but we only have a day. Can we pray before I leave?"

I heard no words as he spoke, for my mind was swirling, dipping and diving through the visions to find the words I would relay to him the next day.

"I want 'Over the Rainbow.' Can Robin sing it? The new version, and 'Amazing Grace.'

"You can choose the rest. Talk to my parents.

"I'll give the eulogy. I am his mother. It has to be me.

"The eulogy has to be before the songs. I won't be able to talk afterward.

"We will receive friends, have a private reception, not in the news.

"In the obituary…" I paused with that word. "In the obituary, ask the media not to come. Out of respect for the family.

"And… let's ask people to bring balls. Ben loved balls. We will donate them to a charity. Also, ask everyone to wear bright clothes to the service. Ben is bright. Black makes no sense."

29

Riley curled up with her head on my lap, the room lit only by faint moonlight breaking through the windows and the flicker of the television before us. Fatigue had set in, and her eyes hung heavily as she slowly fell asleep to the hum of voices and music in the background. Kaylyn lay next to her, leaning into Kyle's body like a pillow. She had long since fallen asleep, her thumb periodically falling out of her mouth.

I had begun to crave this moment at the end of the day, when my mind floated away into the oblivion offered by anxiety and sleeping pills. I sat on the opposite side of the couch from my husband, as if on a perch where I could watch over the roost. I could ensure that, if just for that one glorious moment, all was well. Part of me did not believe Kyle deserved family time yet, which insinuated normalcy, but Kaylyn craved her father's attention and love again. She needed to touch him, lie in his arms, fall asleep there. So I let her, and as I noticed the joy it brought both of them, I became increasingly annoyed at the fact that a state agency was trying to keep them apart. From healing together, where they naturally needed to be.

We did follow the rules the first few nights, with Kyle sleeping in the in-law suite while I took the king size bed with the girls. My mind could not slough off the *what ifs* that intruded periodically. What if he were to awaken from a dream and lash out at the body next to him. What if he were to roll over in a stupor and smother her. Of course, she was eight at the time and that was nearly impossible, but my mind would imagine the impossible for years to come. It was not the ordinary that had killed my son. Yet the nights were becoming more of a struggle than a consolation, with Kaylyn pitching a fit to sleep with her father. I finally relented and agreed to break the rules.

The first night I allowed the two of them to sleep in the same bed, I began to dream again. Vivid, lifelike dreams. Kyle and I stood together, suit and flowing white wedding dress, in the church of my childhood in South Carolina. A sanctuary of family and friends surrounded us. My mind focused on a vision of green in the front row. A woman sat, watching as if in a deep peace, beautiful brown curly hair cut short atop her head, vibrant green dress flowing in the breeze. She seemed satisfied, content to observe without interacting. No one else appeared to think it abnormal that she was there, as if she was invisible to everyone but me. She appeared healthy and alive, though I knew she was not. Then I was whisked forward in time to Connecticut, where I stood by the door of my car, looking into the backseat. I watched as a strange woman breastfed Ben. His hands touched her skin, just like they had so often touched mine. It seemed so easy for her, the simple act of mothering. I looked away in resignation. I was powerless and useless. I felt as if I was an unfit mother.

30

Shelly, my best friend, arrived on Thursday. Short black hair, quirky glasses against her Persian features. A glint in her eyes, with a smile. The usual attire she wore to all of our weekend get-togethers. Striped shirt, jeans, and sneakers, hiding the fact that she had been a manager at a Fortune 500 company for years, only recently retiring to the South to be a stay-at-home mother. We were yin and yang, and she brought with her a temperament that fought to avoid outward displays of emotion. "Stop. Don't make me cry," she would often say in the upcoming days. Instead, she tended toward sarcasm and laughter, which I desperately needed. Seeing her demeanor, that it was acceptable to act like that around me, allowed others to do the same. Crouched around the island in Jen's kitchen, planning a funeral, we were allowed to laugh and cry, often at the same time.

She had offered to take Ben's clothes to the funeral home on Friday, something I could not bear to do. To look through clothes, to hand them over to the funeral director. It did not make logical sense to me. Baby clothes. Funeral home. Burial. I raced frantically around the house, overturning suitcases. Where were his sandals? I needed them. Not substitutes, only the blue sandals, with small holes where I could see his toes. Sand would get inside, I had to shake it out.

"Don't worry, Lindsey. I'll go buy some," she had assured me.

I would one day find his blue sandals in the bottom of a suitcase and feel a sense of relief wash over me. Glad that I still had them, for those shoes were Ben. There were memories in the scuffs, which I could keep with me forever.

*****

"You're not going to believe what happened to me!" Shelly announced as she walked back into the house after her visit to the funeral home. Her eyes glistened with mischief, a slight grin on her face. We all looked at her questioningly.

A red Mercedes had passed her several times as she walked down the side street to the funeral home. A man was driving, and he watched her as she walked. "I'm sure he just thought I was hot," she said, glancing up to ensure we were smiling, "and he probably *wasn't* following me, but I thought he was from the media." After exiting the funeral home, she hastily marched down Main Street into Tazza, the coffee shop we had frequented together every weekend, where they knew her. "I need a hat and apron," she announced, "I'm being followed." With questioning looks, they handed the disguise over to her as she snuck out the back door to her car.

"I felt like a spy on a secret mission," she informed us. "It was so much fun!"

The room was lifted by laughter as we had to lean against the island to keep from falling. There was laughter and there was love, and in that moment, nothing else mattered.

31

My feet hit the hardwood floor with a clop as I threw the sheets across the bed. I was stunned and reeling, awakening from a dreamless sleep the day of the funeral with a sudden electricity and terror pulsating through my body. Riley lay on her side in the bed, snoring soundly beneath crumpled sheets.

"Oh my god, oh my god," I said out loud, gasping for breath.

"What's wrong, Mommy?" Riley inquired, rubbing her eyes and peering at me through strands of hair still falling haphazardly across her face.

I tried to reassure her as I fumbled to find my phone.

"Mom, I didn't get to say goodbye!" I shrieked into the phone, hyperventilating. "I need to see him again. I can't do this!"

I analyzed the lines of tendons and bones pushing and pulling in conjunction as my bare feet paced across the smooth, polished floor. A focus on the warm, pink flesh of the living only reinforcing the reality of the coolness of the earth that would crumble beneath the force of shovels later in the day. I had put it off until it was unavoidable, acknowledging this punctuation mark of death. The moment of no return, when the reality of loss was inevitable. I saw his skin, plump and healthy like mine, slightly relenting beneath my fingertips as I caressed his cheeks in sleep. Skin to skin. Dust to dust.

Since I had decided I didn't really want to know if God was real, and I was not satisfied that I would ever see him again, the memory of a living Ben, held in my arms, was all that remained. The look, feel, smell, sound of the Ben who was, and I was not ready to say goodbye.

When my mother arrived at the house an hour later, I asked her to drive me to the mall. I needed something to connect us, something for Ben to keep. I found it in a jewelry store, a blue heart, split in two. One side engraved *Mother*, the other side *Son*.

He can take a piece of me with him, I thought, *and I get a piece of him.*

"Is this for a birthday or birth?" the clerk asked.

"No, my son died." A relief washed over me from the honesty. I wanted others to know without truly having to understand. There is death. On a perfect summer day.

She blushed, gushing apologies.

As we walked through the mass of bodies in the mall, a thought began to percolate of why it was so integral for me to see Ben. The shock the night of his death had been too overwhelming for me to say a proper goodbye, and I was not ready to let him go without seeing the flesh of him one last time—but there was more. I kept envisioning Kyle opening the car door and finding his son. He had seen his son dead, a picture that would haunt him for life. I felt helpless. I could not take away his burden, but I could share it.

"Can you handle that?" my mother asked.

I was not sure, but I did know I was not ready to bury my son yet. I needed to see his face one last time. I was not ready for him to become only a memory.

32

The familiar smell of the funeral home finally solidified the fact that I had lost a child. It was not a casual grief. It provoked wrath. My eyesight tunneled through the hallway before me to focus on the form of the funeral director standing near a table at the end. He wore a dark suit and stood with his hands clasped in front of him. Flowers lined the hallway beneath large mirrors, outlined in gold. I felt as if the walls were crumbling to the ground as I walked toward him, relenting beneath the weight of unadulterated reality. When I reached his side, nothing was left except the words floating between us.

"Where is he?" I asked in preparation.

"He's in that room," the funeral director answered, pointing over my left shoulder. "Are you ready?"

"Yes."

I told Michele she could wait in the hallway. I needed to do this alone. She complied, reminding me she would be there if needed. I shook my head and followed him into the room.

The room was too big for the tiny white casket pushed up against the far wall. It was bare, with rows of brown folding chairs in the center. I avoided looking directly at the casket, as if it were a blinding light. I could only experience the moment by dissecting it into pieces. The movement of my legs, the funeral director's hand on my elbow. A sense of the casket in my periphery, safely out of sight. A bare wall, painted yellow. I felt as if I were sidling up to something dangerous. Sidling up to death, to embrace it.

He guided me toward the left. *A misdirection*, I thought. I followed, but my eyes remained averted. With a magnetic repulsion, I pulled away from him. "I'm not ready yet," I said out loud. I knew what I saw would remain indelible in my memory forever, and part of me wanted it to—as punishment. I wanted to hurt myself, and this was the surest way.

"It's fine. Take your time," he responded with care.

I backed up to the casket, eyes still fixed on the bare wall, painted yellow. I would have to do it suddenly and quickly. I had hoped to touch him, kiss his forehead, spend minutes telling him all the things I had not gotten to say. "I love you, Ben, so very much. I miss you." I would place the charm engraved *Mother* in his hands.

But when I turned, I knew it was a false hope. I was again inside myself, in a pool of darkness and infinite time. Nothing I had learned, in church or textbooks or philosophy, could describe the truth of what I saw and felt in that instant. Nothing was left but a deep whirlpool of yearning.

I covered my face and turned around immediately, howling through sobs, "That's not him. That's not Ben!" I did not understand. He was gone. That was not him. I quickly gave the charm to the funeral director and asked him to please place it in the casket with him. "I can't do it," I cried, walking away.

No words captured what I had seen. It was just a body with no soul present, which means there is a soul that can leave. It was not him, which means that whatever comprised *him* was more than a body. You and I are more than bodies. He was tiny, not bursting with the breath of life, which means there is a breath of life, of something more than this, that exists. Yet it was his eyes that I missed the most. Closed in death, their essence seemed to have disappeared.

I raced out and collapsed into Michele's arms. "I have to leave." I rushed out the back door, running from what I did not know. She followed and we stood outside in the afternoon heat fighting back tears. No words. Only the sound of sorrow.

I would remember his eyes during his lifetime and wonder. What had they seen, into what world had their essence fled? Had they seen God and followed, and was it so stunning that he had carried its beauty in his eyes all his life? Was it him, in the ocean of deep blue, all along asking me to simply look and finally see?

33

When the procession arrived at the gravesite, our small group of friends and family stood waiting. A sea of black. As Kyle received their hugs, the stone mask of catatonia began to melt for the first time. With each touch, he became more human.

"We can't start yet," I said, my eyes searching up the street. "Someone isn't here." I needed him there. It was Shelly's husband, Phil, who was Ben's unofficial godfather.

"He flew in today. He's on his way," Shelly whispered as she hugged me.

We were standing in a bookstore when I told them. We had just met a few weeks prior, but they noticed I was refusing to drink a glass of wine. Newly minted friends, joking. "Are you pregnant or something?" I had denied it at first until the next morning during our weekly coffee date, but it was just five weeks, so still early, I told them. A year later, we sat around their kitchen table as our daughters watched a movie, talking and laughing. Ben grunted as he army crawled around the kitchen floor. Phil got down on all fours, face to face, talking to him. Ben grinned and chuckled, grabbing his nose. "He loves that boy," Shelly had said.

My eyes remained fixed on the horizon until I saw the black town car pull into the cemetery. It was not real until I saw him. His face would serve as confirmation, and when he stepped out of the car, reality fell like bricks. Ben really was dead. We were changed forever. Phil emerged from the car, short dark hair, black suit, sunglasses covering foggy eyes of grief. His face was forlorn, holding back tears. I collapsed on his shoulder, crying. "Ben is dead," I said and heard a stifled sniffle, but no words in response. I understood. There were no words, just the experience of Ben and God, on that day, in the emotions we all had.

Kyle and I took our places with the girls in the front row. I stared at the stark white casket and the blue flower arrangement flowing over the edges, as if by analyzing its contours I could actually believe my son lay inside. There was silence, only the sporadic buzz of insects nearby, and the sound of cars in the distance. My mind danced outside of my body as the pastor spoke. I heard only the drone of his voice and sniffles behind me. I continued to examine the casket, which housed the flesh of my body. Light reflected off its smooth surface as dragonflies flew from one flower to the next. The deafening sounds of the day were broken by an uncontrollable sobbing. It was Kaylyn, who had yet to cry after her brother's death. As Kyle rolled her up onto his lap, I knew this was her time. She had to grieve in order to let go.

When the pastor ceased speaking, I took it as a cue the service had concluded. In the silence, no one moved, as if they were waiting for a signal. I felt as if I were a string puppet, dangled precariously in the midst of another mother's life, expected to perform the necessary rituals of mourning, but nothing was real or natural about this day, and I only wanted to leave. I stood, kissed my fingers, and touched the casket, thinking that was an appropriate action. It was all a ruse, the thought that there would be a calm saying of goodbyes, a gentle letting go. I stood to the side of the canopy and mumbled some phrases—thanking everyone for coming, inviting them to our house, relieving them of their duty to watch the burial of a child. No one should have to bear that burden.

As I stood with Kyle and the girls, waiting for everyone to rise and leave, I noticed they were not following my instructions. My skin tingled with an uncomfortable energy as I watched the scene unfolding before me. Of other humans and their hearts, needing to linger just a moment longer. As our car pulled away from the cemetery, others stood unmoving. They would stand together transfixed by a single blue-green iridescent dragonfly that remained, a still calmness of recognition atop the gravesite marker. The blue ribbon on the flower arrangement flapping in the breeze. Benjamin Jacob Seitz, brother, beloved son.

34

"Benjamin, son of my right hand," I began. "According to the Old Testament, Benjamin's mother, Rachel, died in childbirth after a hard labor, calling him 'Benoni' in her last moments, or 'son of my sorrow.' His father, Jacob, later changed his name to Benjamin, he being the youngest of his twelve sons."

As I scanned the sanctuary for familiar faces, I grappled with the import of his name. He was to be my last child, too. He was the son of my joy, yet in that instant alone, he was the son of my sorrow. I felt a heavy weight on my shoulders as I searched the eyes staring back at me. I measured the slump of their shoulders and placement of their hands in their laps, trying to ascertain what they needed from me. If it was strength, I was not sure I had any to offer. Or possibly this was the moment when I must feign strength, in order to become it. Maybe the bodies before me were my secret motivation. Support them in order to support myself.

The eulogy I pinched between my fingers began to shake. I focused on the top of the typed page, where I had handwritten in pencil the words *Slow, Breathe, Be Strong* with the symbol of a cross and heart doodled while deep in thought. My knees weakened, and I focused on the sense of Michele and Shelly standing behind me. My heart fluttered. I knew what the congregation needed, just not whether I could deliver. They needed hope. That love could survive death, that we could all survive the impossible. That there was something more than the wooden seats beneath them, stifled tears, red faces.

I had sat on Jen's patio writing the eulogy the day prior. *There is a core*, I had thought, *a core of something I need to convey.* It was coursing through my body, in my very blood and bones. An experience for which there was no description. "**We had a lot of fun with his name because we soon realized you could pair so many things with Ben… it was Benjabear, Benjabuddy… but ultimately, he is just my sweet baby boy, Ben.**"

The hot, tempestuous yearning that had attached itself to me through death. The love and skin and flesh that we only have for a sliver of time. *That's it*, I had thought, *I'm seeking an iteration of love and time.* "**He was the typical third child, not your normal boy yet. Yes, he was getting very independent and opinionated, but I called him tender. He wasn't rough. He touched things with tenderness, including my heart.**"

The moment is here, and then it is gone. It hangs in the balance as it passes, like the trembling of leaves in the wind, and you cannot call it out of the depths once it falls. You have only the darkness and the memories. So use it wisely. "**He was chill. He was quiet. He smiled and laughed. All. The. Time.**"

It is in the laughter and the smiles and the hugs that hurt. First words and last kisses. "**Most things don't matter, but this does. Part of his love for life was his love for nature, dogs, sports, and… yes… balls. The little toddler running around 850 Degrees pizza restaurant with the beach ball during the World Cup soccer game parties, laughing—that was my Ben, and yes, that was me running after him. Those are the moments.**"

I wanted to shake them awake to make them understand what I knew now, but I had only the words on the paper before me, which would never be enough. "**My sweet, sweet Ben.**"

I could not tell them that life would never fall apart before their eyes. I was standing before them as evidence of that. "**In the end of** the novel *Farewell to Arms,* Hemingway writes 'The world breaks everyone, then afterward many are strong at the broken places.'"[2]

Yet there was the core of something greater which would usher you through. Love and God and family, all three merging into something altogether new and indescribable. Words that could never convey the power we all harnessed. There is a love that cannot be destroyed, and you will hold on and strain and fight and scream, and you will survive. "**We will be stronger in the broken places. We love and miss you, Ben.**"

My muscles released when it was over. I had just shared something personal and could not bear to look into the sanctuary to witness the results. I felt bare and raw and only wanted to hide once more. My quick glance as I walked down the steps to the nearest pew showed eyes no longer staring at the floor, hands grasping the closest loved one. A new lightness was in the air, an ephemeral sense that we could all survive death together.

As I took my seat, Riley climbed on my lap. White sundress flowing over my legs. As the deep tonal breadth of "Amazing Grace" enveloped us, not a sound could be heard in the church absent the deeply powerful sobs of a child. It was her turn to mourn, to say goodbye.

By the time we made our way to form the receiving line, my brain had reverted back to the dreamlike state in which it hibernated in times of overstimulation or anxiety. The line of friends and family walking by slowly turned into a mere blur of forms, offering handshakes, hugs, condolences. I shook my head and complied. Mumbled words in response, until it all began to disappear.

I handed out tiny slips of paper with the location of our private reception. "We're trying to avoid media," I stated as an explanation. As two dozen or so families filed into a friend's house, I walked from one room to another until I found my way to the front porch, where I stood silently, listening to the laughter and screams of children playing soccer in the yard.

My mind had already taken me to another world, wherever Ben was.

35

Spring 2003

"But I want to have children," I informed my psychiatrist during a regular session. I watched the dust particles illuminated by the light from the window behind her. I could not look at her, to witness her reaction. I wanted to give her a moment for it to sink in.

"Okay," she responded, slowly, carefully picking her words.

I could imagine her weighing the next steps. *Don't send her off the deep end again*, I am sure she warned herself. She needed to offer me some semblance of hope.

I felt like an unsolvable paradox. I was bipolar, but I was also just me, so what did that all mean? Who was the "I" in that sentence? I wanted to have children. Educated and loving me, but depressed and suicidal me. It was unchangeable, and fighting against it was only making it worse.

"I need to talk to someone about it because I have questions," I had continued. "I don't want to get pregnant right now, but I need to get this all straight in my head."

It was part of the process of trying to come to terms with myself, which I was never able to do. Was my life over? Was I a normal member of society? Was my dream of a family, large Christmas dinners, and grandchildren an illusion now?

She found a specialist for me, a perinatologist who worked with the mentally ill, of which I was now one. We met in a small room within Duke University Hospital and were joined by a resident. We all sat, legs crossed, eyeing each other, waiting for the first move. I was enveloped by a plague of insecurity, an insecurity that would chase me throughout my life. What were they thinking without saying because it was not professional? Were they stereotyping me? Did they really believe the mentally ill should not procreate? That there should be no more evolution of us?

The doctor prodded me. Why was I there? I knew they had already read my file, but it was a standard ice breaker, as if by making me say the words, I could be healed. It was a multifaceted question. Why was I here, in general? I had been questioning for over a year and already concluded maybe I should never have been born. My illness was a blight on humanity. It added nothing but pain. Why was I here, specifically? I was bipolar; it was pretty bad, but I wanted to have children one day and needed to know if it was possible. Also, could my children get my illness? I had heard it was genetic.

I cringed, fearing judgment, and wondered if they would relay to me just the facts, not garnished with opinion, or layer opinion beneath facts. I was not sure anyone without a mental illness could decide whether it is worth the risk of life and love. Whether there was any beauty in loving someone through suffering.

She took my second question first.

"Yes, there is evidence that bipolar is hereditary. Studies vary, but we generally understand that there is about a twenty percent chance of a child having the illness if one parent does, compared to around four percent in the general population. With two bipolar parents, it is even higher, but that doesn't mean your child would have it, and there is just no way to tell. It is about risk."[3]

"But how could I get pregnant cycling like this?"

"Well, with the severity of your illness, being a rapid cycler who sways between hypomania and depression quickly, along with mixed states where hypomania and depression exist together, you would absolutely need to be on medication during your pregnancy. It seems lithium is working well for you so far. Correct?"

"Yes, if you don't include the fact that I'm losing chunks of hair, my hands shake, and sometimes my speech is slurred." Did that mean it was working well for me? The bitterness and sarcasm that formed my worldview was also exuded in my speech.

"Right, but it is stabilizing you, Mrs. Seitz. Lithium is a pregnancy class D drug. There is an increased risk of a severe heart defect using lithium during pregnancy, but it is rare. With the severity of your symptoms, I would recommend you stay on it. Surgeries can correct the heart defect. The benefits would outweigh the risks for you personally."

So I was supposed to stay on a toxic medication, risking my child's heart, all to save my own mental health?

"You need to remember, the postpartum periods are worse for women with bipolar. You will need to be on medication."

"So should I just not have kids?" I asked bluntly. *Just say it,* I thought.

"We can't answer that question for you," she responded blankly. "Many women have done it, but there are risks. It would be very difficult for you."

I leaned back, squaring her up with my eyes. *I know what you want to say,* I thought, but I remained silent, allowing the flood of fear, insecurity, and guilt to wash over me.

36

They are questioning the wrong person, I had begun to believe. I found myself sitting on the ottoman across from my husband and Bob. *It's all me, not him. Can't you see that?* I thought. The seeds of personal guilt had finally begun to bloom in full array. We had been given a weekend respite to mourn and bury our son, but now we were thrown back into reality, forcing us to tread water furiously, and we were drowning.

Bob had advised against allowing Kyle to give an in-person interview, and we agreed. Nothing could be gained from that. If the state's attorney was going to charge him, he would do it with or without an interview, and with his mental state, it was not smart. So underneath the lamp light on that Wednesday night, the three of us sat drafting a statement of my husband's guilt or innocence but not mine. The law governs logical causation, not the abstract. It would not follow the chain of causation back to the small room at Duke University Hospital, where I had first made the decision that love was worth the pain. That there would be a Kaylyn, a Riley, and a Ben. They've got the wrong person, my heart screamed. I should have never had children. My simple existence created Ben, and I felt unworthy of being a parent.

We were drafting a statement of facts. He forgot his normal turn. He turned right at the next intersection instead. He got coffee. He drove to work. We missed all the signs. The moments poured like rain, but they never flowed backward, into the past, into my life, where I eternally placed the blame.

*****

The perinatologist had been correct. I denied the inevitable during the good times, when I was reasonably stable. It was a misdiagnosis. I couldn't possibly be bipolar, I kept telling myself. Until it hit and I sat in another doctor's office telling her. "I guess I do have manic depression." The crevasses in my psyche kept reappearing, often merely from lack of sleep or extreme stress, but always during postpartum periods as my mind slowly fell into a deep darkness. Yet they had said it was possible to have children, and that was the only opening I needed. I had to try, and we had learned how to manage it, partially, until I would break again. There would be a changing of career paths or jobs, loss of friends, often moves from state to state.

There was a madness after Ben's birth, as if in the form of a known grief. A mother's rage of loss and longing, felt in reverse, as if his becoming had begun the cycle of my unbecoming. Had some part of me always felt the love and loss of him? Did it reach even further into the past? Was the loss of him part of the agitation I felt those lonely nights in North Carolina, weighing my options? Pacing in hospital rooms? Had I broken so severely and so often early on so I could be strong now when it really mattered?

Four months into this last postpartum period, I had sat in our pediatrician's office with naked, chubby Ben grinning from ear to ear, giggling, as I informed her that I was done breastfeeding. "He is obviously very healthy, and it's time for me to transition to formula so I can get back on medication. I'm really struggling," I informed her. I was not a mother like this. Kyle and I had tried to squeeze as many months out of it as we could, with him carrying on most of the parental duties so I could rest. Ben slept in a pack-n-play beside our bed, and when he cried at night, it was Kyle who went to him. Paced and rocked him. I slept in the girls' room, waiting to be awoken every two hours for feedings. Bits of sleep. Here and there. It was the best we could cobble together, and it worked, until the darkness returned. I always told myself I would catch it this time before it got bad, but the plan inevitably backfired. I could not catch something early that I did not accept even existed.

Investigators would later ask us about the days leading up to Ben's death. No, we did not do drugs. We had not been drinking the day or night prior. "They will want to know how you remember that so specifically," Bob warned me that night, beneath the lamplight. I remember because on the day before Ben died, we were tired. It was not just an immediate tiredness either, but a bone-gripping tiredness. The tiredness of a lifetime together, of struggles and sleepless nights, of imperfection and love. Of holding on when it would have been easier to let go. So as we navigated the parameters of causation that night, I retched inwardly. It was me; it was always me. I looked at my husband, gaunt and pale. His fault was only that he loved me.

37

In the first few days after Ben's death, news reporters had gathered on the steps at the local police station, rabid and waiting for more news. "Why is it taking so long?" they asked. "We want names." Articles were written, our house was shown on the six o'clock news, comments and opinions flew through social media. Local community members quoted in articles, strangers cloaked in anonymity commenting online with presumptions and calls for prosecution. *Their kids mean nothing to them. We all know he should be charged; people like that should never have kids. The smell of their car. The little white casket. Don't assume he's suffering; he didn't love Ben. He should suffer more, and the mom, she shows no emotion to the public, she probably helped him do it. She's an attorney, an easy life of privilege. Her career means more than her children.*

My emotions were raw, and I only wanted to fight, to stand at the top of the stairs and scream for the world to leave us alone. To protect my family. It was instinctive, a gut reaction to the world that appeared to be circling us with swords and daggers, but I knew it was wrong. I could not present myself as such, nor would I want to. I had to think and breathe before I reacted.

Over time, I became addicted to the feeling of simply waiting and being still. It became my drug. It was the only power I had left in a world that was quickly crumbling beneath my feet. I would breathe and find a calmness before acting. I would make others wait, allow them to act as they wanted. I relinquished any hope of controlling others and realized I could only control myself.

I thought of my favorite book, *Man's Search for Meaning*, by psychotherapist Viktor Frankl, a survivor of the Holocaust. He had written of his times in concentration camps in an attempt to discern the characteristics that enabled some prisoners to survive while others could not. Survivors had found some meaning in suffering, whether it was contemplation of loved ones or the simple act of holding on to the most basic of human freedoms. He found that "everything can be taken from a man but one thing: the last of the human freedoms—to choose one's attitude in any given set of circumstances, to choose one's own way."[4] Prisoners retained the spiritual freedom to choose the attitudes they would embody, and it was in that simple act I found the only bit of peace I had in a single day.

I often felt as if the ingredients that made me human were gradually being stripped away, one by one. I had lost my son, my parental rights were in question, my husband's physical freedom was an unknown, and the very core of my being, my mental illness, was now under intense examination. Our private lives were public information. I had lost all control over my environment—investigators, prosecutors, the media— and lacking that, I only felt helpless and inhuman.

I had one thing left—the ability to control my own thoughts and actions. My reactions, my energy. It fed an insatiable hunger to retain some sense of humanness, and as the days passed, to turn the pain into something positive. To choose my response, to take negative energy we received, mold it, and send it back out into the world as something positive. I'd felt the pain of being on the receiving end, and I could not bear to do the same. I would often fail, for my pain and anger remained just that, but I hoped to succeed more often than I failed.

38

Bob was certain Kyle would be charged. I still hung onto a naïve thread of hope. I did have my fears, though. It would be easy for me to judge the prosecutors and presume what I would have done in their circumstances, but I could not be so glib. In fact, I was not so sure myself. My husband had, in fact, forgotten our son. It was a hectic morning, and he missed his normal turn. I often told myself I would not have forgotten Ben, that I could not be so mentally absent, but somewhere deep inside, I knew it could have been me. Still, part of me did blame him. I would always blame him. His actions, or lack thereof, had proximately caused my son to die.

    I understood the psychology behind it and had sat for hours researching the phenomenon in the weeks after Ben's death. I thought of the many times I had found myself standing in our bedroom, knowing I had walked up there to retrieve something but forgetting what. Pulling into the parking lot at work, not remembering my drive over. The cracks form when habitual memory, which controls actions that one performs regularly, takes over for prospective memory, which controls the purposeful planning of actions in the future. Kyle had planned to take Ben to daycare, on a route he drove each day, then to coffee, then to work. There had been a glitch. A moment that I would never be able to understand or describe, but it did occur.

    Those aspects could all be debated in court, but I found myself mulling over another issue on countless occasions. Regardless of whether there was an action of fault in fact, there was the question of whether, under any theory of punishment, any good would be gained by criminal prosecution. Should he be incapacitated to protect our family or society in general? Did he need to be rehabilitated through punishment, drug treatment, or other interventions? I could answer those questions in the negative.

Could his punishment deter future hot car deaths? I wavered on this idea, as it depended on too many factors. Could it deter parents from talking or texting on their phones while driving or prevent other negligent acts, which could lead to forgetfulness? Possibly, but Kyle had not engaged in any of those acts while driving that morning. Could punishment teach others to live in the moment in a hectic world, or was his act of forgetting too utterly human for that? I was unsure.

Lastly, was punishment just if it served only as pure retribution? *Make him suffer more*, I had thought that first night in the emergency room, but I had also seen the depths of his already-existing soul-wrenching suffering. As he had expressed, no one could punish him more, and prosecution would reach beyond him to everyone in our family. His children could lose a father, his potential for employment to support them could be affected, or he could lose his own life from depression. So what was justice?

I would have felt more comfortable if I could simply say I would not have charged him, but I could not. I was an attorney and knew how I viewed my responsibilities. I had taken an oath to serve my client, and my client alone. More abstract ethical theories addressed my duties to adversaries and society at large, but client service was my mainstay. Working in a prosecutor's office in my twenties had given me ample opportunity to see the role of politics and statistics in prosecutions. State's attorneys are elected in most states, and to win you must be well-liked with a high conviction rate. It is in our bones to fight and win. It is built into the structure of our occupation.

Bob had put his feelers out, just to see what the inclination was around town, whether he was right, and Kyle would be charged, or if we would be allowed to heal in peace. The consensus had focused on the political nature of most government decision-making. There was pressure on both sides, to punish Kyle and to set him free, there was no right answer. "The state won't take the heat for not charging Kyle. The state's attorney will probably just put it in the court's hands, leave it up to a jury. That is the easiest decision. It takes the pressure off them," he ultimately concluded. "Plus," he said, head tilted toward me, "his actions resulted in a death." They could charge him because they truly believe he committed a crime and deserves to be punished more than he already is. The question is whether it rises to the level of criminal negligence, versus civil negligence. Do the specific facts make it a crime?[5]

As I looked at him with a blank stare and contemplated our future, I felt a rising uncertainty. If I could not rest assured of my own actions, I could not predict the future actions of third parties. Kyle may indeed be prosecuted, and our lives may continue to crumble.

39

Dusk was arriving by the time we lit Kyle's birthday cake, the last day of July. I felt our past in the shadows of the trees lining the beach area. Ben had sat in the sand at the foot of the picnic table, cross legged with knees in the air, feet not quite touching. A little girl with blonde hair braided over her shoulders had sat across from him on her knees, tossing his favorite inflatable basketball in the air. *He is so happy learning to play with other children*, I remember thinking, as I watched her roll the ball to him. He giggled, picked the ball up, and threw it back to her. A bubble of joy was created by their game, surrounding their bodies. No adults could break into their world. He looked back at me with dimpled cheeks.

We all knew we could not recreate the lightheartedness of the past, but we wanted to see Kyle smile again, even if forced and artificial. A group of friends had gathered around, singing "Happy Birthday." He let a shy smile escape, tinged with the forlorn. The kids stood off to the side, screaming, "Are ya one? Are ya two? Are ya three?" all the way up to thirty-six. We laughed as they scattered to drag their kayaks back into the water before the sun set.

"Hey, Lindsey, Ben wants to take the kayak out after the girls," my friend Sharleen, sitting beside me, stated simply.

It happened so suddenly, an inward gasp not only of my breath but of my soul. I could neither inhale, nor exhale. Time stopped, coalescing into one instant where he was alive again, sitting beside the picnic table and tossing a ball. Ben rushed in to fill the gaping hole within my heart, only to be ripped out again when the moment passed. I covered my mouth with shaking hands, responding frantically.

"You said Ben," I whispered.

I thought she had misspoken, calling her son Ben by accident. The physical pain then began to grow. Tears flowed. I realized my mistake. Another Ben was at the beach, and not my Ben.

My Ben was no more.

Later that night, Kyle and I walked off behind the trees and sat on the shore of the lake, hidden from view, leaning against an overturned kayak. I let him put his arm around me for the first time since Ben's death, allowing myself to fall into him. "I miss him so much." The essence of grief held in the simplicity of the statement. We cried together, children laughing in the background, watching the tiny ripples of the lake carry us farther and farther away from shore.

40

We were seated on the porch of Farmer & the Fish, a white eighteenth-century house turned into a restaurant in the neighboring town. Ferns hung down from the rafters, vibrant colors of petunias, salvia, and begonias in the flower garden in front twisting around the building to the two acres of farmland in the back. It reminded me of the Southern farms of my youth, a wide covered porch where you found three generations of women in rocking chairs, cups of iced tea in their hands. Friends with two girls of their own had cajoled us out of the house for brunch. It was August 3, a clear summer day, one of the first times Kyle had ventured out in public. He sat beside me on the bench. We made sure to sit with our backs facing most of the patrons, hoping no one would recognize us. I sensed a nervousness in his mannerisms, as if he was struggling to uncover the parameters of appropriate behavior around others. A smile or a laugh often followed by a downward slant of his face, as if in shame.

We allowed the girls to play in the side yard while we ordered so we could talk freely. The juxtaposition of the beauty around us and our heavy hearts was obvious to our friends, who tried their best to keep the conversation flowing. I found myself sitting in silence for long intervals, interjecting here and there. We discussed our upcoming sabbatical to Colorado, and then Texas, where we would be spending some time with our friend's father-in-law, Stan, on his ranch. We sensed a battle approaching, we told them, and needed some time alone to gather our strength and begin the process of healing. I watched mouths move as they responded, but my mind had drifted off in thought, overcome by the constant terror that was mine alone.

I had learned quickly that the sweep of DCF's investigation reached far beyond my husband's parenting abilities and actions the day Ben died. DCF was investigating me as well.

"Mrs. Seitz, when I asked you yesterday whether there was a history of mental illness, you said no. However, we have been informed that you suffer from manic depression," Jason stated, a cool edge of accusation. Our pediatrician had told them when questioned if there was anything DCF needed to know. I would question later, in anger and sadness, why my pediatrician had thought my mental illness was relevant in the investigation of my husband, ultimately resigning myself to the fact that misunderstanding and stigma grow deep.

I had thought he was only inquiring about my husband's mental state the day we first met. I was not involved in any events related to Ben's death. "I don't see why you need to know my personal information that had nothing to do with what happened," I responded.

"Ma'am, we have to make a full assessment of both parents in cases like this. Your information will be kept confidential," he explained further.

I cringed. "I don't want this information to be leaked to the public," I reiterated. *It could ruin me,* I thought.

He had hit upon that part of me that I kept locked away inside a hardened heart. A ghost of me that cried and moaned, rattling the cage bars, wanting only to be free. Its piercing screams of discord vibrating through me. I would never let anyone have this part of me, but there was more to my resistance than that. I had a legal right to medical privacy, to keep some aspects of my life as mine alone. I understood that if DCF was asking me to relinquish that right, they would do the same to others. People just like me, with their own hidden ghosts. They too had a right not to be judged, not to be stigmatized. I felt a need to stand up for the privacy rights of us all. It was the only human act I felt I had left. The remainder of my humanness had been stripped bare. I could regain some control over my life.

I gave him the basics to answer his question. If he did not have my medical records, I had no need to go further, and I still held firm to the stance that my private medical history was not relevant. I had a physical illness of the mind, a disability, but on that day, like many others, I had been stable. Guilt by association would not stand up in court, and I could not allow my privacy to be invaded due to the acts of another person—my husband.

I informed him I had been diagnosed with bipolar disorder in my twenties. I had been consistent in taking medication when needed and complying with treatment, leading a largely successful and stable life since then other than episodes of darkness during postpartum periods. I offered my doctor's name and prescribed medication.

"I'm the most stable person in the family right now," I said strongly. In this crisis, I was the strongest, and I felt a pride in that. A small success amid a lifetime of failures.

"We need a release of your mental health records and to speak with your doctor," he stated, assuming compliance.

"No," I stated, my response instantaneous and ingrained. "I will get her to write you a letter describing my treatment."

"That's fine," he said as his demeanor softened. "That is usually enough. We just need it for the file. Make sure she specifies your treatment and any concerns."

I could not yet comprehend the reality that, through an investigation, they were building a case against me too, of questions and doubts and innuendos, which would have to be allayed before peace could return to our lives. That even through silence, they would find doubt. I had asked my parents to stand strong and protect my privacy as well, and when questioned, they pleaded ignorance, referring Jason back to me for information on the topic of my mental illness. In the record, Jason would describe every look my parents gave each other before answering, their reluctance in talking about my illness. He would insinuate secrets in silence. Something nefarious.

When Jason called me a few days after I submitted the letter from my psychiatrist, I finally realized something deeper was evolving, from higher up in DCF. "The letter isn't enough. We need a full release of your medical records and to talk to your doctor," he informed me.

"Why?" I asked.

"We need a full assessment of the family. We need to ensure you are capable of taking care of the children, considering your husband's state."

"The letter tells you I am compliant with treatment and attending all of my office visits, and my psychiatrist has no concerns over my ability to care for my girls," I stated, "and you have talked to many others involved with our family right now to gather evidence." However, it was not enough.

"It's not going to happen. Next question."

The words fell like stones in my memory, until the girls' voices, ringing with excitement, brought me out of my head. "Mommy, daddy, a bird laid an egg! You've got to see this!"

I placed my hand on Kyle's shoulder as I stood, insinuating that he could stay. I would go play with the kids. I followed them to the side of the restaurant, where several wooden posts stood amid rows of flowers and small green bushes. The lushness of nature overtook me, and I allowed it. I fingered through the bushes, searching for a nest inside.

"No, look mommy, down there!" the girls screamed in unison. "I saw the bird land on that post and something fell out of it. I thought it had gone to the bathroom or something. But… it laid an egg! Right here on the ground!" Kaylyn jumped up and down, pointing.

There, lying unbroken at the bottom of the post, was a robin's egg. Blue and still. Over my left shoulder, the robin stood perched on the fence bordering the property. Watching. Silent. I felt something magical pulling at my heart, as if Ben was hiding just around the side of the building, giggling and saying, "Hey, Mommy, I'm right here!"

"You are not going to believe what just happened," I proclaimed as I returned to the table and explained the kids' discovery. We smiled, chuckled, and continued talking about our vacation into the wild beyond. The wide-open spaces of Colorado were beckoning us, and we felt an urgent need to escape the world around us, if just for a few weeks. As I sat there watching the tension fade from Kyle's face, I felt the screams of bitter discord within me begin to weaken too, and in that space was placed a tiny key by a little boy, with eyes of ocean blue. As if he were indeed just around the corner, giving me hope.

PART TWO

41

I could smell history in the red sandstone as we stepped out of our car at Garden of the Gods in Colorado Springs, Colorado, on August 7. I felt within myself the same friction and turmoil of the masses that had caused these formations some sixty-five million years prior. A gradual uplifting and simultaneous erosion of grief and earth. They stood towering before us, emanating an accumulated energy that enveloped me. It reached beyond my body, as if part of me were merging with the sun and sky. Kyle and I lagged behind the girls as they ran ahead squealing to climb the smaller rocks. "Be careful!" I warned them, my protective instincts run awry. Our perceptions were overwrought with sensation. The mystical freshness of red clay mixing with the sagebrush and wildflowers. The sweet wind tunneling off the peaks and the absence of civilization.

I had come to Colorado to find my way back to Ben, and it was there, scanning the vista before me, that I first felt him, or God, or both as one. In a gentle release of tension into the transcendent evening air, we stood on the rocks overlooking the nearby mountains. An exhale of pain, inhale of air brimming with energy and possibility. I felt my body melting away as I became part of the earth, sun setting, faintness of stars appearing above. I could gather no words, so I stood, alone and still, until tears formed as evidence of my emotions.

I felt a gentle hand touch my leg. "Mommy, can I hug you?" Riley asked softly.

I kneeled down on the dusty earth and complied.

"I just miss Ben so much sometimes," I told her.

"Me too, Mommy."

"How do I get through this?"

She placed her forehead against mine and grabbed the sides of my head with two small five-year-old hands. "Just stay calm and stay with me. Let me love you. Because I am your sidekick," and that night, as I cried myself to sleep in her arms and she rubbed my face with her delicate hand, she released another part of me into the night sky. "It's okay, Mommy... accidents happen." I had found unconditional love in the red clay of the earth. I had felt for the first time as if Ben were here, and then he was everywhere.

42

I want to know what you know.

Atop Pikes Peak, the clouds surrounded us at eye level. At once, I felt a sense of being a part of the earth, observing it, touching it, but also of being far removed from the body of it and the limitations of its pain and suffering. As if in one step, I could exist far above, floating weightless, looking down, shadows of minutiae below. The sunlight gently nudging my shoulder. A reminder to look up.

I want to see what you see.

The feeling was an impossibility I could not fathom. That he lay in the clouds before me, droplets of mist levitating in the air, light rays interspersed between. So close yet so far away. I felt our hands outreached, toward one another, yet unable to transgress the infinity between here and there.

I want to hear what you hear.

Kyle felt it too as I watched him in the distance, alone, shoulders shaking from tears atop Pikes Peak.

"I'm so sorry, Ben," he said to nothing but the blue sky, and altocumulus clouds speckled gray.

We could take a step forward and know what you know, but we remain inexplicably grounded by the rocky outcropping beneath our feet. Firmly with the living.

On our descent, I understood I was not ready to leave Colorado, not quite yet. It was the gentle nudge of sunlight on my shoulder. Some beauty in the living. In the ability to touch the love of Ben through nerves and skin. I looked up as birds soared above. Free. I will stay, one day more, maybe two. To continue feeling the beauty of red sandstone, rolling mountains of the Rockies.

43

Luscious pines rose on each side of Cheyenne Canyon, the city in the distance. Pockets of summer heat flowing through the canyon and across my body. Hawks flying through the valley, spanning the distance between the two mountains like a tightrope. We could hear the roar of Helen Hunt Falls below us as we hiked the switchbacks to the scenic overlook. It had been a steep ascent in the heat, and I stopped periodically for Riley to rest and gulp down some water. I glanced back at her crouching in the stream nearby, looking for rocks to take back home with us. Mica. I'd told her to look for something shiny in its depths. I stood on the scenic overlook running my fingers across the plaque in front of me. An inscription caught my eye: *M + B 12/31/2013*. I thought of Ben, Mom + Ben. The year of Ben.

I heard voices approaching to interrupt my solitude and called Riley out of the stream for pictures. "Can we talk to Ben?" I asked her. "He can hear us; he's all around us," I explained as we stood together, my arms wrapped around her tiny body.

"Okay," she responded slowly, unsure.

"Let's tell him we love and miss him. No one is around," I offered, as she giggled.

"We love you, Ben! We miss you!" The breeze carried the echoes of a mother and child across the canyon, as my pain merged with the earth around me.

This is God's country. I could live and die here, I thought as we sat in a restaurant at Denver International Airport, awaiting our flight to join the rest of the family in San Antonio, Texas. It was the first impulse I had to run from the darkness of our life back east to the sun and earth in Colorado, and it brought with it a sudden sense of physical loss and longing. I did not know how to maneuver around the question of whether I could bring Ben with me if we moved. A pulse of anxiety coursed through my body. It was a concept I had never had to contemplate before. I knew it was only his physical body, that the spirit of Ben was now all around me, wherever I went. I had felt him just yesterday, and I still sensed an invisible string connecting my heart to his. I had to be near him. It felt more natural to talk to him directly, not in the starlit skies. We would have to start planning.

We arrived in San Antonio three hours later. The airplane cab door opened to torrid waves of heat emanating off black pavement. Stan had invited us to his house as a respite from our lives back east. He lived on a large ranch outside the city, and we arrived just in time to get settled in for dinner. He had custom designed the house to make use of the land's own natural beauty and gifts. The double-layered back porches spanned the entirety of the house, built in such a position as to tunnel the Gulf winds on sweltering afternoons. The porches faced the west to capture sunsets of golden red. The vista before us appearing more as an African savanna than the Texas desert. Massive oak trees splattered across the canvas along with tumbleweed and sporadic fishing ponds.

I would spend days reading and writing on the porch, listening to the laughter of the rest of the family in the pool below. I had always wanted to take the family on a safari, and we felt as if we had finally arrived. Yet something was missing, and as the days progressed, the emptiness in my chest began to grow. We ended each day with a nice dinner and wine, laughter and conversation, but I could not ignore the void that now existed within me. Something was indeed missing, gone forever. And that was the reality of death.

44

A deck had been built on the top floor of the house, an outcropping of attic space. Partially enclosed, partially open air for star-gazing. I often made my way up there after dinner. I found a kind of solace there in the dark of night. A puzzle board of lights before my eyes. This night the void had reached unbearable proportions. It tugged and ripped at my soul. The stars were brilliant yet unmoving, as if to mock my attempts of finding answers within their patterns.

As I gazed into the sky, I begged gravity to pull me to the depths. Break me, free me, let the shattered pieces of my spirit fly unmoored to the heavens, but the earth could have my body. I lay on my back on the rooftop patio, sensing that I was united with the stars, Earth, and universe, spinning endlessly. My mind, turning circles around the moment, convoluted from the night's attempts at forgetfulness, provided a false sense that my wish was being granted. I felt my body sinking deeper, being pulled further and further away from the heavens. Yet the patchwork of smooth, cold tiles pushed hard against my back. I was unmoved.

As I spoke to no one, or Ben, or God, my tongue caught on the dry, bitter aftertaste of the pinot noir that would never numb the pain. The strong night wind off the savanna tunneling in through the breezeway brought with it the smell of the giant oaks, towering in the distance during the light of day, only shadows in the moonlight, along with the sweet juice of the cacti merged with salt air from the Gulf nearly two hundred miles away. The wind caressed my face, and as the tail of each wisp left my skin, I could almost smell the faintest musky scent intertwined with baby powder in the night air. Taunting me.

My ears picked up the slightest rustle of leaves, a whispered hush of tendrils rubbing against one another, a language all of its own. The melody of a single bird in the distance, a sound seemingly misplaced in the darkness, a specter too out of place to be meaningless. Is that Ben saying, "I'm here," I wondered, listening to the clang of glassware downstairs in the kitchen sifting up to my perch from the open window. I remembered the moments when that sound spoke of merriment. Of joy and friends.

As my eyes passed from the silhouettes of the oak trees in the distance to the deep, black night sky, a flashing red light floated quickly across the periphery of my vision. *That is real,* I thought. The metal and engines and stewardesses walking down carpeted aisles and the pop of each drink for waiting hands. But where was Ben? Since his death, I had felt him, but that night, amid the infinite void above, there was nothing. I felt he was so far away from me. I visualized the stars, planets, to the ends of space, if that even existed. He had once been real, but what was he, where was he, in that moment?

The silence of the gusting wind was broken by the patio door creaking open. *Please leave me alone,* I thought. *Tonight is not the night you want to walk out on this patio.*

"There you are! Everyone has been looking for you," Kyle said as the door shut behind him. He walked over to the edge of the balcony nearest my feet, safely out of sight. "What are you doing? Are you okay?"

Tears ran down my cheeks, dribbling onto the cold slabs. An energy pulsed through my body—muscles, bone, heart, brain, blood coursing loudly through my veins—vibrating with the power of the night, pulling and yearning to be reunited with Ben. Yet as I looked into the sky, I found nothing. In the space between the stars, only emptiness and the shuttle of metal and engines.

Rolling to one side to stand up, my eyes met his. Tall, sunburned from days in the sun with the girls on the ranch, a thin portion of the man I knew just two months before, his muscles stood strong, but the weight of his body conveyed the truth. His eyes were dead, part of his soul left with Ben. Lines etched in his face, begun by years of laughter, chiseled in the end by pain and self-punishment. It would have been understandable to have said (and meant) "I hate you," but the truth was really not that simple.

I stood facing him, feeling the unimaginable emptiness of the night settle into my chest. "Am I okay?" I began slowly, sarcasm sliding off my tongue.

"You forgot my son, left him alone to scream and cry, wondering why we weren't there to save him. He burned to death in a car!" I screamed, my eyes shooting a heated venom, the only antidote long since blown away by the wind.

He stood silently, head tilted down, taking it as sought-after punishment.

"I had no choice in the matter! You aren't God. How can you unilaterally take my son away from me?"

I looked up at the constellations once more, watching the red light of the airplane disappear slowly over the horizon. "I miss Ben so much it physically hurts. I want to jump off the side of this railing. My body needs to hold him and he's gone. There is no God. There is nothing." I heaved from the deepest portions of my belly, my scream turning into sobs of pain. "You had no right to do this!"

He looked into my eyes, tears streaming.

"There is absolutely nothing you can say. Leave me alone." As I turned to hold tightly to the railing, I heard the door slam behind him. I was alone, bathing in the stillness of the night, hands grasping metal firmly to keep me there. I leaned forward over the railing into the tantalizing darkness below. A fleeting instinct to simply let go. I turned my gaze once more to the barrenness above as the void bore holes in my chest, which was pounding with pain. I turned, allowing my back to slide down the stone barrier. I remained crouched, arms around legs, shedding tears of impossibility.

45

The day had seemed like an anomaly, effortless and calm, as if we had turned a corner of sorts. The heat had released its grip, foreshadowing the changing seasons. We spread our blanket out on the cushion of green grass at Ballard Park, back in Ridgefield, books anchoring the edges. I watched as Kaylyn strode across the field, sinewy legs rotating like a locomotive, tan skin from our recent trip out west. The bright orange ringed Frisbee arced through the air over her head, landing on her outstretched arm like a horseshoe game. She screamed with glee, "Ah ha-ha, I got it!" Kyle stood a good twenty yards behind her, smiling. We all felt it, as if a weight had been lifted for the day.

Darkness had fallen as I stood by the window in our sunroom, the ringing of my phone bringing me out of my daze of reminiscence.

"I've got bad news," Bob said.

I could sense my own seasons changing as I read the tone of his voice. Anxiety coursed through my bones. "Oh no, what now?" I asked.

"I received a courtesy call today from Susan Robertson, assistant attorney general (AAG), notifying me that they are filing a neglect petition against you and Kyle in the superior court for juvenile matters."

Blood puddled at my feet as my head began to spin.

"Just against Kyle. Right?" I prodded.

"No, you too. You are the other parent. Listen, I'm advising you to get your own attorney."

"What?" I exclaimed. "I didn't do anything!"

There was a pause. And static.

"Yes, you did. You didn't give them what they wanted, and they'll try to force you to do it," he explained.

"What do they want? I've met them halfway."

"Halfway isn't good enough, Lindsey. They still want a full release of your mental health records, and they aren't backing down on a full forensic interview with the girls."

"They are not getting my girls," I responded. "Let them take me to court."

"They are trying to threaten you, and they will do it until you break. You need an attorney to bridge the gap between you and them. You are an attorney and mom; you need a neutral party."

"I've got to go." I heard Bob calling my name as I hung up the phone, throwing it onto our kitchen table and walking through the hallway toward the front door. Kyle had overheard the conversation, catching me at the door as I tied the laces of my running shoes.

"Where are you going? What's wrong?" he asked.

"DCF is taking *me* to court now too!" I screamed. "I can't do this. I need to get out of the house."

My trot picked up speed as I crossed our yard onto the gravel driveway leading to the street. Kyle would expect me to turn left, so I veered off to the right. As I jogged up the steep hill by our house, I glanced down at my attire and was shocked by the absurdity of the scene drivers would encounter along the road. A woman sprinting down deserted streets at ten o'clock at night, hair pulled back in a ponytail, capri pants, sweater tied to her waist, old beaten running shoes. I hadn't taken the time to change. *I have finally become that grieving mother,* I thought, *the one that finally just loses it.* I glanced back toward our driveway to ensure I was not being followed. I felt the structure of my known reality quickly dissolving before my eyes, and I knew no other option than to escape into the darkness of the night, alone with only my thoughts and a beating heart. I was out of shape and hoped if I ran fast enough, my heart would just stop, for in that moment, I could come up with no better option.

The path was pitch black, with no streetlights on the rural New England road. Tears blurred my view of the shoulder, so I raced down the center. As I crested the hill at the top of our street to turn left toward town, I felt my heart pounding in my chest. I sped up, for it would have to beat even faster in order to relinquish its hold on life. I was not sure where my feet would lead me. I only knew I could not stop moving. I relished the opportunity to lessen my pain as I watched headlights approach every few minutes. It would only take a fleeting moment of weakness. Music blasted through my headphones, covering the sound of my guttural sobbing and gasping breath. "Ben, oh my God, Ben," I groaned.

My thoughts matched the quick cadence of my feet against the pavement, racing to process the events that had unfolded that day. As if by pondering them long enough, I could unravel them, rearrange them in an order and form that made sense.

"The letter from the girls' psychologist is not enough," Jason had informed me in late July. "We want our own forensic interview." I envisioned the room, each girl alone, in turn, a table for them to sit across from a psychologist they did not know, asking questions that need not be asked, toys lying on shelves around them. Closed doors, investigators watching behind panes of glass. I had been informed that parents were not typically allowed to even watch. They would be alone.

"Why? They see their own psychologist that they know. They are comfortable around her. She's told you they are doing well. You are not going to continue traumatizing them. They are happy and moving on. You have evidence of that."

"We have our own set of questions we would ask that your psychologist may not."

"Like what? If we beat them, if we are drunks? Or are you trying to find out more about that day?"

"It's not like that. It will be an open dialogue with our own psychologist."

"What if you submit your questions to us, and our psychologist can ask them?"

"That won't work."

"Why not?"

"Listen, do you want to talk to our psychologist and ask her your questions?"

"Yes. Then I'll think about it."

As I continued to sprint toward town, I noticed headlights bearing full speed toward me around the corner. I immediately crouched behind a tree on the side of the road. I was not ready to be found. The pieces still lay around me in disarray.

The forensic psychologist called me five minutes later.

"You know our situation. Correct?" I had asked her.

"Yes, ma'am. Let me tell you first that I am not an employee of DCF. I am an independent contractor, and I am only talking to you because they asked me to."

Okay, okay, calm down; she sounds more reasonable, I had told myself as I paced through our front yard.

"What do they use you for then? In what kinds of circumstances?" I asked.

"I am a forensic psychologist. They use me in court. I also interview children, usually ones who are abused or have witnessed a death or other trauma."

"Well, that doesn't apply here. So why do we need you? We've submitted letters from our personal psychologist."

"I don't know, ma'am. They just called me in."

"So what? You are supposed to ask them if we are abusive? I don't want my children to be alone in a room with a stranger. They are loved, well-adjusted children. I don't want them to ever know that a parent would beat a child or that there is so much pain in the world." There would be time for that, one day, but not now. I wanted them to remain innocent for as long as I could help it. For Ben's death and its aftermath to be a detour in their life of grief and sadness but not a change in its trajectory. Not a trauma. To create a bubble around them, keeping their lives as normal as they had been before his death.

"No, it would be more of a symbiotic dialogue than that."

"So you would ask them to talk about that day again?"

"Possibly."

"They are already past it. They are laughing again." I paused. I could sense tension across the line. "So do you have kids? If you were me, what would you do?"

"Mrs. Seitz, I have four children. My advice to you as a mother and attorney is just to do what you feel comfortable with. That's my advice."

I had heard enough. I thanked her and hung up the phone.

Bob had argued to allow DCF to speak with the girls. "They'll have nothing but great things to say about Kyle," he told me.

"That's not the point," I replied. I ran him through my logic. We had already offered letters from the girls' personal psychologist outlining her findings that they were openly talking about their brother's death and healing in a healthy manner with no apparent problems. If DCF was concerned about the girls' grieving process or mental health, we would provide them with evidence that we were adequately caring for their needs through our own psychologist. If this was not enough, that was the only indication I needed that the interview with a forensic psychologist was geared toward something else, whether gathering eye-witness testimony of the day of Ben's death or trying to dig deeper into our parenting styles to weed out any forms of neglect. Goals that would be achieved through strangers talking alone with the girls about issues that they would not understand or *need* to understand at their age. They would be forced once again to discuss a tragic day from which they were already expressing a need to move on. A judge should have to rule with a court order that an interview was warranted given the evidence presented, I ultimately concluded. I had been told early on there may come a point where Kyle's interests and mine would not align, and I was sure I had found that point.

I called Jason back immediately. "It's not going to happen," I said firmly. I was exhausted from trying to negotiate and had given up trying. They would take the action they needed, but it was out of my hands.

My legs were beginning to buckle as I neared town. The pounding of my feet had not beaten any form of recognition into my life, only confusion and disbelief. When I finally took my eyes off the road, I saw the cemetery looming before me. Shadows of massive oak trees draped like curtains over rows of small, arched gravestones. A desolate silence comforted me. There I could exist anonymous and alone with nothing but my pounding heart and burning lungs.

I slowed down to a walk, looking for the most private place to expunge my demons. I shuffled over to a large mausoleum to the left, collapsing behind one of its ten-foot-high walls. By the time I leaned my back against the cool cement and tucked my legs underneath my arms, I had surrendered.

"I can't do this. I simply can't. We can't survive *this*. Please help me," I cried to Ben, tears wetting the sleeves of my shirt.

There was no response, only silence beneath the moonlight. I lifted my gaze to find a bench in front of me, a tribute to a three-year-old son, inscribed: "With infinite maternal love. 'A little child shall lead them.' Isaiah 11:6."

I stood in the darkness and walked helplessly to Ben's gravesite, stretching out over his body. The ground was moist from the recent rain. A coolness soaked through to my skin. I wanted to float away into the night sky, become the glittering stillness of the stars. Far removed from the reality of the earth, destined to exist unmoving yet resolute.

"I love you, Ben. I miss you. Please, please help me. I can't do this alone," I repeated until I saw headlights reflecting off of the glossy finish of the nearest gravestone. Kyle had finally found me; he had come to take me home.

46

Thick humidity mixed with the chill of the night as we stood together at the base of the Washington Monument, craning our necks to look up. The night was black with only the lights of the National Mall and Lincoln Memorial breaking through like beacons. As we walked along the side of the Reflecting Pool, Kyle took my hand, and for the first time since Ben's death, I did not shy away. I felt the depth and grit of history in my bones as we walked the steps of the Lincoln Memorial. We took a seat off to the side where we could be alone and watch the radiance of a full moon break through the clouds above the monument in the distance.

The anatomy of that moment gave me hope. That the impossible had been done before. That there was a strength in unity, a power in conviction. Something in the very air we breathed that night was worth fighting for. I settled into my own body and allowed him to pull me closer. Not a word passed between us. We did not have to speak to relay what we both felt.

Earlier that night, we had eaten together on the patio of a little Mexican restaurant off the beaten path, mesmerized by the sounds of the city closing down at dusk. A flock of warblers passing over the stone building towering to our right. The sky turning powder blue, tinged with sapphire clouds. That night we had felt as if we could fall into the cloak of our old lives, back when life was much simpler, sharing a date night out, laughing, talking about the future. There was possibility in the night air.

We had come to Washington, DC, to speak with senators and the Department of Transportation about child vehicle safety, but the trip offered us more than that.[6] It was the first time we had been alone since Ben died. Anonymous, in a city that carried within its structure the beauty of antiquity. It was not the first time we had laughed and felt a slight release in tension. We had begun to forget our current reality in tiny fragments of time, falling back into our old lives if but for an instant. These moments were usually instigated by the girls, but this time it had come just through us. In the darkness of the night, in a foreign city, we had found a space to hide, away from the world, and we crawled inside like two lovers reunited after a lengthy separation. Tentative and shy.

*****

Four score and seven years ago our fathers brought forth on this continent, a new nation, conceived in Liberty and dedicated to the proposition that all men are created equal.

That night, as we had stood at the foot of the statue of Abraham Lincoln, the words of the "Gettysburg Address" brought a tightness to my chest. As I looked up at the engraving on the wall, I was finally able to put words to the general uneasiness I had felt over the past two months. It was based on the social contract embedded in the very marble beneath my feet. I had forgotten what it truly meant to be an American. Here, I am free. Citizens are equal in the eyes of the law. In building our society, its founders consented to surrender some of their freedoms, to be ruled by an external authority, in exchange for the protection of their remaining, natural rights. I submit to authority, but it must be a just authority. An authority that can only take away my most fundamental rights if I have broken my side of the contract. It is a country in which I cannot simply wake up one day and as a result of no wrong act of mine be subjected to a complete degradation of my rights and all I hold dear.

And I held my family dearest to my heart. I was a good parent. I provided for my children, I supported their hopes and dreams, and I loved them unconditionally. They had been raised in a household where they held a deep-seated security in our love. The girls were more than a part of my life. They *were* my life. Every waking moment that I was not working, I was with them. Kyle had been a stay-at-home dad when I worked in New York City and had only returned to work at a local engineering firm when Ben was four months old. Our children were a part of us and went everywhere with us. It was more than love; we were a part of each other, and as parents, we were their world. Yet I had woken up one summer day and had it all called into question, through no act of my own. I was no longer free.

I had drawn a bad lot. I suffered from a mental illness. I struggled from day to day at times, but I had overcome the brunt of my illness to live a high-functioning life. I had graduated from law school and performed well during my career as an attorney. I had battled through one postpartum depression after the next to parent successful children. I was even able to hide most of my symptoms from my children. However, I felt anything but equal in the eyes of the law. I felt neglectful until proven otherwise. I felt stereotyped.

As I finished reading the inscription, a rising unrest spread through my body. I knew it would be easiest to just give in, but I had to hold on. I found a relief in finding something to believe in, during a time when I no longer felt human. I believed in my right to privacy of my personal medical records in a case where the state had no evidence my illness negatively affected my children's care.[7] I believed in my parental right to make decisions that affected my daughters' best interests. Who they were forced to talk to, what topics were introduced to their still-forming brains, the ethics and morals that would surround them. I was still their mother, and I was not willing to let go of that honor so easily. So I would fight to keep my private struggles where they needed to be, hidden in the past.

47

Fall 2004

Chalk screeched as the professor finished his masterpiece, tiny pinwheels of benzene molecules moving in a blur as he slid the blackboard to the side with a crack, an empty canvas appearing from beneath. Air vents pulsated loudly above my head; seats squeaked as fidgeting bodies swiveled the chairs beneath them. I sat mesmerized by the beauty of the organic reactions, the patterns of the living. Yet I wanted to be anything but part of the living, part of the complex combinations of symbols and charges being fervently scribbled on the board, gyrating and merging before my eyes. Most of us were pre-med with plans and a future, but I just wanted the class to be over. I squirmed anxiously in my seat. Sweat formed.

As the mass of students tumbled out of the classroom, I engaged in mindless conversation with fellow classmates, pretending, and then rushed off to my car. Pictures from various textbooks danced in my head as I walked. Electrons, clouds of potential existence, here and there, and nowhere at once. Bulb-like synapses of the brain, globe-shaped neurotransmitters floating from one to the next. Serotonin. Dopamine. These molecules were within me too, and they were failing me. I had sat through weeks of monotony, organic chemistry, biology, physics lessons crystallizing with rapid speed in my mind, then as quickly as they came, disappearing into a whorl of confusion.

If I paid close enough attention, I could feel the synapses misfiring in my own brain. Often too slow, sometimes mismatched and foggy, other times frenzied until my mind fell into a blur of motion. Centrifugal. Over the course of two years, I would drop out of classes more than once, giving my professors one of many excuses. There is an illness in the family. I have to travel back home this semester. I felt my own life turn into a cloud of potential, existing here and there and nowhere at once.

In the darkest days of agitation, attempts at studying had turned into bouts of complete mental uselessness. I often sat hidden in a corner of a coffee shop on Main Street in Chapel Hill, textbooks, spiral notebooks and novels piled on the tabletop to form a barricade of sorts, coffee steaming in my hand. I had to keep my mind busy, and if I could not concentrate on studying, I would turn to reading. In the beginning stages, I could devour one to two books a day depending on the length, until gradually the sentences merged into each other and words fell apart, leaving only letters and the space between. The doctors were slow to settle on the proper diagnosis. "It's just a dark depression," they had said initially and offered one antidepressant after another, but I only got worse. Then they had tried mood stabilizers, finally settling on lithium. Depakote was not as efficacious for me, and the potential liver disease had scared me enough to ask for another treatment protocol.[8] I felt like a test subject, abnormal, inhuman.

On Wednesday nights, I sat with fellow outpatients around a small conference table in an office at Duke, blackboard at the front of the room, fluorescent lights turned on low, a small lamp in the corner. We huddled around the table together, as if sharing some kind of secret. Something mysterious. We were all equipped with workbooks for cognitive behavioral therapy. With practice, we could link our thoughts and feelings with our behaviors, end the pattern of self-destruction. "You could teach this class, you know," the instructor said jokingly one night as the others eyed me across the table, since I was a compliant patient and high functioning. She did not know I was only the master of deception. That my mind was dissecting the words and phrases on the board into letters, creating a language of its own. Hypomania loosened the cogs of my brain, allowing a flood of thoughts from every aspect of my life to flow into the room at once. *I'm creating a theory! A theory of everything!* I almost screamed out loud, but I remained silent, for letting the others in on my secret would reveal my utter mania. I worried they would believe me to be crazy and I would be hospitalized again. Mine was a madness beyond haunting. I hid it well.

When I arrived at our small apartment, I rummaged through the dresser drawer where I had hidden a cornucopia of medications. Bottles of mood stabilizers and anti-psychotics, whose side effects had caused them to be tossed aside with a hot aversion. Knowing a stash lay so close to me at night carried with it a comfort. I was addicted to the option of death.

*****

My green Jeep Cherokee sat parked behind a dumpster on the adjacent property, unnoticeable from the road or parking lot of the hotel. I did not look the hotel clerk in the eye as I handed him the cash for the room and gave him a false name. I fingered the cell phone in my pocket book, ensuring it was turned off, what I thought to be untraceable. I made a joke. We both laughed. I needed to feel human one last time. Upon entering the room, I placed all of my contraband on one of the twin beds. I stood at the foot of the bed, silently examining the remains of my life before me. A bottle of red wine sat on the nightstand. It was not dark enough. I could not die in daylight, I thought, grabbing a handful of cash and the room key. I would eat. Before walking to the closest fast food restaurant next door, I took several antipsychotics to calm my nerves, topping them off with a glass of wine.

As the wine and medication began to mix, my mind spiraled out of reality with visions of my elderly relatives, long passed, popping into and out of existence. They sat at the tables near the glass wall, leaning in toward each other as if in deep conversation. They avoided eye contact, but I could feel their awareness of my presence. They were watching me in other ways. White haired and aged, each of them looked just as they had the last time I had seen them, but effervescent. It was an essence of them, not physical bodies that I could analyze and grasp. They were not eating or talking, seemingly undisturbed by my arrival, as if I had always been stuck in time, arriving there.

The servers eyed me as I walked through the line, the drug cocktail noticeably affecting my demeanor. I periodically glanced over my shoulder toward the wall. "Do you see them?" I wanted to ask. "They are dead." I felt an immense peace and comfort, as if I was finally home again. The moments of my life on the farm, happy and loved, stood enmeshed in my mind. I had an urge to cry. "I miss you all so much. I love you," I wanted to say out loud to no one but the servers who were staring.

I sat at a table nearby, watching them as they simply existed unmoving, and ignoring me. I tried to grab their attention, walking to the trash can beside their table. Still nothing as I left to return to the hotel.

While crossing the parking lot, I fell. A man ran to help me up. "Are you okay?" he asked, as I stood, blood pouring from my knee, jeans torn but no pain. "Yes," I responded and continued walking. *What does that even mean, am I okay?* I wondered. I bought a Snickers from the hotel clerk and returned to the room. It was time.

48

I stood in the hotel bathroom wiping the blood off my knee, examining the skin through torn fabric. *It doesn't matter*, I thought. I felt no physical pain.

How complex it was, the will to live, in its most elementary form. Seed-like. So small, yet so ingrained it had become unnoticeable. It was more than a fear of death, of nothingness, or the unknown, or roulette. It was the unrecognizable desire to be more, to be deeper, to be involved. To experience more than the concept of love and pain, forgiveness and anger, but to *be* a part of it all, through tissue and blood and nerves and heart. Even in suffering. Even more in suffering. To do more than observe, and through the act of being, to grow toward something greater.

Suicide is an act of desperation, an exasperation with life. It is the critical temperature at which hope of recovery (of a life without pain) begins to boil, unruly and tempestuous. And to reach this critical point, I had to counteract the will to live that had sunk its claws deep into my psyche. I would slip into death slowly, with one pill at a time, allowing each ample time to drown out any hope that remained.

The pills began to dissolve with an acrid taste on my tongue before I swallowed. I paused to pace. Paused to ensure my phone was off, then placed in a drawer. Waited for the fog to grow thicker. It needed to weigh heavily upon the seed, like a blanket of snow. *I don't want to die. Yes, you do.* Voices, one overcoming the other, in unison. I sat down on the bed, took a few large handfuls and slowly drifted off in a stupor.

Hours later, I sifted through a dream. I heard knocking. "Open the door," voices said forcefully. I heard the door opening, sensed forms walking toward my bed. Many forms, more talking, and I felt hands against my body. The fog was thick, and as one layer of dream gave way to another, I lunged toward the night stand. *The fog is heavy. It's here. I just want to die,* I thought as they carried me away.

49

"Hey, honey. You're back?" Carol asked disappointed. "I was sure they'd gotten your medication right the last time." I realized I was becoming a frequent flyer as I shuffled through the hallway in slip-resistant socks and hospital clothes, a nurse's hand on my elbow. My body relaxed with the familiar smell of the lemon surface cleaner and Carol's concerned yet comforting face. Round with slits for eyes, broad cheeks grinning back at me. Here I felt safe. I was home. We passed the multipurpose room on the right, where we would be eating our meals and attending art and group therapy. A few patients mingled around. One elderly woman with curly white hair and wide-rimmed glasses sat motionless in a stupor on the sofa, facing but not watching the television. I wondered what medication they had her on so I could avoid it.

Further down the hallway, we passed an open area on the left, one of the two community rooms for television and meetings with visitors. A talk show ran in the background. Two patients played cards on an end table. Our eyes met, causing mine to immediately return to watching the rhythmic movement of my blue socks.

"Here's your room," the nurse informed me as she wrote her name on the white board and began to sift through my bag, confiscating any contraband. I knew what not to bring by this point: no razors, sharp objects, belts, or items with any chemicals. I would be wearing my glasses for the extent of this visit; they took nearly everything else. "You are on twenty-four-hour watch, so I'll be with you nonstop for a while," she informed me. *Great, I can't even pee alone*, I thought. I knew it would evolve into suicide watch, which was different in that I would earn privacy for fifteen-minute intervals before the nurse popped her head into the room again. I looked forward to that bit of respite.

I walked into the bathroom, nauseated from the charcoal I had been given to counteract the overdose. The bathroom was bare, much like the remainder of the room. No hangers for towels, no shower curtain, sterile. There were bed sheets but nowhere to hang myself. She watched as I urinated. I tried to avoid eye contact. My brain was still fuzzy. I simply wanted to sleep. As I crawled into bed, pulling the sheets over my head, the nurse took her seat in the chair against the wall, magazine in hand.

The psychiatrist made his rounds later in the day, followed by a flock of residents and medical students. I despised this part, and my mind involuntarily convulsed. A jury of my peers, learning through me, talking about me behind closed doors, judging me. I felt an impulse to tell them they were no different than me, but I refrained. I used sarcasm to combat my feelings of inadequacy and annoyance as they prodded me with the same questions over and over again. Freudian glimpses into my childhood. Trauma. Family history. Socioeconomic, educational, and marital status. Sexual practices, drug and alcohol use. Medication history.

"So what happened, Lindsey?" one asked.

"You know what happened. It's in your file."

"But I want you to tell me. Did you want to die?"

"I don't know."

"What do you mean you don't know?"

"I don't want to live like this. I want to be able to die, yes." *But I'd prefer for you to make me better*, I thought but decided not to say.

"What have the past weeks been like for you?"

I stood up and began pacing from the bed to the wall, and back again. *Don't look at me like you know anything about me*, I thought. I assessed the tiny barred window and cement walls before responding.

"Fucking agitated, manic, depressed. I can't sit still. I can't think. I just drive and drive to nowhere trying to calm down and figure out what to do. My hair is falling out from the lithium. My hands shake, and I don't want to live like this anymore. It's not human."

"Okay, so what other medications have you tried?" This time the psychiatrist stepped in. "It sounds like you could be rapid cycling on top of your mixed states. Do you know what that means?"

"Yes, I know what *that means*." Disgust and frustration were building. "I'm not stupid." I took a breath and listed my medication history for the group. I had memorized the speech. During one of my first stays at Duke, I had stood in a room around the corner about five doors down, examining and pulling apart the spiral wire in my writing journal. If I could only get it out, I would have a mode to end it all. I threw the notebook across the room exasperated, realizing the Zoloft had made me too unstable to accomplish even that simple task. "Help me!" I'd exclaimed in desperation, marching into the hallway and up to the nurse's desk.

"But that was when they thought I was just depressed." I remembered the first time I was hospitalized. The Celexa my outpatient doctor prescribed for me had initiated a mood I could only describe as being most akin to pure mania, one so relentless that I could only laugh and joke endlessly. I felt no emotion. I could not even cry.

"Right, well we know you are manic depressive now. Antidepressants only exacerbated your symptoms, so we are on the right track. What about antipsychotics or other mood stabilizers?" he asked me further.

I remembered staring at my form in the bathroom mirror, examining the blue pill in my hand. Psychotic. Anti-psychotic. I felt a reckoning with the words. Swallowing was a kind of initiation. *I am officially crazy*, I had thought.

"The first night I took Risperdal I woke up from a dream and started hitting my husband, screaming at him." Realizing my mistake, I raced into the bathroom to sit on the toilet, hands combing through my hair. My legs twitched. "And involuntary muscle movements." Seroquel put me in the state much like the elderly woman I'd seen in the multipurpose room. Just staring, mouth hung open like a hungry bird. Watching but not seeing.

"What about Lamictal?" he asked.

"Oh my gosh," I responded with a sigh. "It made me break out in the rash. The bad one that means you are having a severe allergic reaction. My psychiatrist took me off of it ASAP."

The flock of doctors and students stopped taking notes to glance at each other briefly. They agreed to go consult and come see me the next day with more options.

"We'll call your doctor, but for now let's keep you on the lithium. It may still be the best option for you, and we can help manage the side effects. Your nurse will still be checking in on you every few minutes. Okay? Don't worry. We'll get you better." He tried to shake my hand as he exited.

"Fine," I responded, embittered, turning to the wall. Later that night, when the nurse closed the door after a fifteen-minute check, I walked up to the wall and stood, motionless. I relented and leaned my head against the cool cement—hard. The only thought racing through my mind: *Make it stop.*

*****

I often found her sitting in a hump in the corner of the community room. She would come out of the catatonic-like spell I had witnessed on my first night there long enough to cry. It was more like a sobbing for someone or something far away. Something I could not reach or bring to her.

"Are you okay, Ms. Anne?" I asked as I sat in the chair beside her one day.

"No, honey. No, no I'm not," she droned on. "But thank you. You are a sweetie. You look just like Sylvia."

She had a male visitor once in a while, possibly her son or nephew, but no Sylvia.

"Who is Sylvia?" I asked, drawing closer.

"Oh, honey, no one. Don't worry."

It seemed to comfort her when I just sat, speechless, while she cried. She finally grabbed my hand. "I'm fine. You don't have to stay."

I took that as a cue that I was no longer helpful in quieting the pain, that pain of places or people long since gone. As I walked away, I wondered if she would eventually be taken to a long-term care facility or whether she would simply remain in the corner chair, staring at the television, sobbing and alone.

*****

Lines of red and blue paint streamed down as I rubbed a brush delicately across my canvas. With the lithium rising to therapeutic levels, I had slowly emerged from hibernation in my room, joining the other patients for art and group therapy, lunches, and movies. Joseph always sat close to me. A paranoid schizophrenic with shaggy brown hair thrown asunder atop his head. He had let me in on his secret that the FBI was monitoring him through the loudspeakers. For some reason I visualized him walking around his house with a hat of aluminum foil, but if he did, he definitely did not get to bring it with him. Here he had to be just like us. Raw and exposed.

My roommate Jess had arrived a few days after me. Long blonde hair, thin, a few years younger than me. She had refused to talk to me at first—we were on a psychiatric ward after all—but my endless chatter eventually forced her to open up. It was unavoidable. We became friends, sharing stories in the dark when we were supposed to be sleeping like two teenage friends breaking the rules at summer camp. It brought us back to simpler times. She took joy in the fact that she only had depression. Therefore she was saner than me. We agreed we were both saner than most on the ward though, finding peace in that one conclusion.

50

In the ancient Japanese art form of kintsugi, the artist uses gold or silver lacquer to repair broken pottery, with the result being viewed as a work of art. The pottery becomes beautiful through the history of its broken places. The complete form is asked to embrace its flawed parts in an act of aesthetic beauty. In this one act, it exists purely—broken yet complete. During my stay at Duke, I was drawn closer toward recognizing the truth and inevitability of my own broken places. I was sick, and it was not going away. "Think of it just like any other illness, like diabetes or cancer. You have to accept it, to treat it, and live a full life," one resident informed me. Yet, I did not have cancer. I could tell people that. I had a mental illness, and it was isolating. I am alone, I reiterated each day. She looked away, not knowing how to respond.

*****

The tables in the community room looked like those from my lunchroom as a child, and I felt like a child again as the four of us stood giggling, furtive glances out the window to ensure the nurses were not watching.

"Shhh," Tiffany whispered, as she walked over to the stereo on the counter and placed a tape inside. As the music began to drown out the noise in the hallway, we all started to dance. Tiffany was younger than me by a few years, African American, with her hair pulled back on the sides. She grinned, and I grinned back. We had immediately bonded when she was admitted to the psychiatric ward. Much like me, she was in between diagnoses and desperately in need of understanding and friendship. We spent hours talking and slowly found our moods elevated from the connection we formed.

"Live like you were dying," our voices rang, as we gyrated to the beat. I felt the speakers reverberating through my body as I broke out in song, glancing again out the window to ensure no one could see me. When the song climaxed and our voices rang out in unison, I felt a sense of liberation, as if my soul was resonating with something outside my body. We were all connected. We were the same, united, not isolated. As the four of us laughed out loud, if only for an instant, we were a form of art. We were cracked, imperfect, but together as one. We were doing something together, and there was power and peace in that. As I left them a few days later, prescription of lithium in hand, I felt a slight sadness in my chest, as if I was leaving behind that something greater that had kept me alive the week before. They were right there waving to me as I walked out, and I had indeed grown toward them, and with them, until I was part of them.

51

I remembered the smell from my law school years. Aged wood, bound treatises and files combining to create a sense of the austere. Of knowledge, expertise, and justice. Peter leaned back slightly in his chair, legs crossed loosely, holding my file in front of his face. His voice was smooth and calm as he read through the allegations of the petition. I felt as if I could float away on its currents and be guided to safer waters. He towered above me, long, thin face with eyes peering over round glasses that slid slightly down his nose. His frame carrying with it the sense of expertise I lacked. I felt a relief simply sitting across from him and allowed my mind to dissolve into the cadence of his voice.

> *The Petitioner represents that the child is neglected in that the child is being denied proper care and attention, physically, educationally, emotionally, or morally and the child is being permitted to live under conditions, circumstances, or associations injurious to well-being.*

I had already memorized the allegations, having sat on my bed for an hour reading the petition, as if by repetition I could believe it was real. They were now claiming that we were neglecting our daughters by not allowing DCF full access to them and all mental health practitioners involved with the family.[9] Details of my son's state upon arrival, cause of death, my husband's reaction, the smell of our car. Words smattered on paper to prove a point, regardless of their grotesque effect. Waves of nausea and anxiety enveloped my body.

Parents were both offered time and space to view their son, both declined. Mother never inquired of father or daycare as to son's well-being. No mention was made of son.

My newly minted representative, Peter Buzaid, finished reading the petition and threw it on the round mahogany table between us with a *crack*. "So they are doing this to break you, until they get what they want. Plain and simple."

"I'm not going to break," I affirmed.

Parents refused to allow DCF to interview the children or allow them to participate in a forensic interview.

"Well. We'll see," he said. "You're a royal pain in their ass right now. Most people break, and you aren't helping the matter. You need to let me be the one doing the talking from here on out. You are too emotionally involved."

Mother refused to sign a release allowing DCF to consult with her psychiatrist re: her prior diagnosis of bipolar. Mother provided a letter from psychiatrist outlining only her participation.

"Can a judge force me to do what they want? Or can I still just say no and go to jail?" I prodded further. I needed to know options. I needed one of them to be that a state agency could not touch my children, that no one could force me to relinquish my rights to privacy, and that I could go to jail to prevent it.

"Probably, yes, but only if they prove enough to convince the judge to issue a court order.[10] You would be held in contempt if you did not comply."

I also feared they would threaten to file for an order of temporary custody if I did not give them what they wanted. I feared losing my children.

We needed a game plan to move forward. He would meet with the AAG within the week to try and establish a working relationship and ascertain what DCF was really after. We would try to turn this into a true negotiation, not giving the state anything unless they gave us something in return. One last ditch effort at compromise.

"I talked to Bob, and we both agree it is the right move to put this all on you. We will let them know that Kyle is willing to do whatever they want because he is innocent and has nothing to hide."

"Fine," I said. I knew DCF would only use my uncooperativeness as evidence of purported instability due to my mental illness, but I had no other choice. I would hold firm to the concept that cooperation entailed negotiation and compromise, not giving in to unilateral requests.

52

I felt as if we were worlds apart as we sat in silence in the Starbucks parking lot. On opposite sides of a battlefield spattered with land mines. I should have been able to let it go, but my nerves were firing in rapid succession, having recently been primed to defend at all costs. He sat in the driver's seat, hands still placed on the steering wheel, staring at the building in front of us. I positioned myself on the edge of my seat, turning my full body to face him. I needed him to witness the full breadth of the statement that was rising in my chest.

While we were talking in the car earlier that morning, he had driven past our first turn to take the girls to school, choosing instead to turn at the next intersection. It was an innocent decision, but I could not let it go. Having rammed my fist onto the glove compartment of our car, I asked him if that was how Ben had died, and as we sat together in silence, the anger only festered.

"Why couldn't you have just killed yourself?" I screamed. "At least then DCF would leave us alone!"

As soon as the words were released from my lips, I looked away with shame and regret. I was no better than others who had hurt him. I was worse, for I loved him. I knew that my words were sacred to him, that I could cut him deeply through my carelessness, but I could not escape the pain pulsing through my heart and wanted him to hurt like me. The DCF investigation had turned into one traumatic day after another, and my body and mind were finally falling apart. Not only had he caused the death of my son, but he had caused me to lose my own freedom as a mother. Neither my ability to parent nor my mental illness would have ever come into question absent his actions on that one fateful day, and in that moment, I hated him for it.

I glanced up and saw his body release something. Quite possibly that was the moment he gave up. As his head hung low, a tear formed. He could speak only through his body, which said, "I'm sorry. Just let me die." I had broken him.

Days later, even after my profuse apologies of "I'm at wit's end, and I didn't mean it," he admitted he thought I was right.

"The only way they will stop coming after us is if I'm hanging by a rope in the basement, but honestly, the only thing they would regret is that they never got to see me in court or harass us more about the girls, and I refuse to give them the satisfaction."

His statement shocked me, but part of me wondered if it was true.

53

"Here is the second letter from my psychiatrist," I told Peter as I handed it to him across the table. We again sat huddled together in his small conference room with notepads, redwell folders, and papers strewn on the tabletop before us. The hope I had harnessed during our first meeting had slowly dissipated, having been tossed and turned into one large mass of anxiety, which now crystallized in the room. Peter had informed me that we were making little headway, and we hoped this letter would help. It discussed my ability to function at a high level, successfully managing my career as an attorney as well as parenting my children, all despite my illness. It also accentuated the most relevant fact for the investigation:

> *Lindsey is very aware of the possible risks for exacerbating her illness and takes great care of herself and is proactive if she has any concern about symptoms she is experiencing. With the recent death of her son, Lindsey was immediately in touch with me to address her symptom of insomnia and responded well to treatment. Despite the circumstances, she has continued without any exacerbation to her illness. She always places a high priority on her health, and realizes this is essential to performing her daily responsibilities as well as continuing as a supportive and reliable parent. I have never had any concern about Lindsey's ability to care for her children as she is a thoughtful and conscientious parent.*

"We'll see if this helps," he said as he glanced up from reading. "It is a good letter, but they may still push for a full release of all of your mental health records. They want to talk to your psychiatrist on the phone also."

My greatest fear was that they would use any symptoms from my past, regardless of their impact on my parenting abilities, to make a case against me as well and force protective supervision on my family when the girls most desperately needed to move on with their lives. Or worse, try to take away our custodial rights to the girls. *Mother has had severe manic and depressive episodes in past*, I could hear the keys of their computer clicking furiously. *Mother has been suicidal in past. Mother had postpartum depression.* They would not understand that for me, as well as many mentally ill parents, the cross we bear is one of a great internal struggle. That we go to the ends of the earth and beyond to keep our pain internal so we can earn the right to be responsible for another, to love another. Our child. Our flesh and blood. That we would take our own lives before we were a risk to another human being, especially our own children.

"How can they use the mere knowledge of my mental illness as a reason to invade the privacy that is my right by law? Do you know how hard I have fought my whole life to keep my illness private? To live with it only inside my own head?"

"You don't understand though, Lindsey. You and your husband are liabilities for DCF. You don't fit the typical mold of a DCF case. Kyle is a liability because of his actions the day his son died. They substantiated a claim of neglect against him in regards to Ben. You stayed with him, and you have other children still under his care. They seem to be trying to make a case saying that is neglect in and of itself. It would have been easier for them if you had simply taken the kids and divorced him. You are now a liability as well, and because of the way the law works, you are joined in this neglect petition. You have restricted the unfettered access to the children that they are used to having. And… you have a mental illness." He paused, almost sizing me up to see if I could handle reality. "They can't keep taking the heat for child abuse and neglect cases. There is just too much political pressure. Your case is highly politicized at this point. It's in the media everywhere, especially after the recent case in Georgia."[11]

"But this isn't politics. These are human lives," I countered, wheels turning. "I understand if they need to have evidence that I am mentally capable of taking over the child care responsibilities and keeping the girls safe from their father, but they have that. It doesn't have to entail a wholesale relegation of my right to privacy. I'm not being uncooperative; I'm trying to compromise." I pushed my chair back from the table in frustration.

"Yes, they do have it but they want more. Think about it. What they are doing now is asking a court to rule that they have done enough. That they have enough proof that you are capable of taking care of the girls."

"No matter the cost," I stated flatly.

"No matter the cost," he confirmed.

"So basically, what I'm hearing is that all of this could end more easily if I just left Kyle?" I asked. "To protect them from the liability of the girls being in the presence of their father?"

"Yes, that is the message I have received during conversations. It would have helped."

"Do you want to draft up a separation agreement then? We can fake it for now. I will live apart from him. If it will make them leave me and the girls out of this, I'll do it. Maybe it's his turn to fend for himself. He did this after all," I proclaimed, but I didn't mean a word of it. The concept made me feel dirty. I didn't even recognize myself anymore, but the weight of the battle was becoming unbearable.

"No," I corrected myself after a few moments. "I refuse to do that out of principle. No one should be forced to break up a family to gain freedom. It would destroy my children."

"Okay," he responded, "if you are going to stay with him, that's your answer. Plain and simple."

"I love him." *Does that mean nothing*? I wondered. I was lost and floundering.

54

As we sat in the tiny examination room at our pediatrician's office, a tight circle of interests, jockeying to be heard, I realized love was not even part of the equation. Our pediatrician had pulled six aluminum chairs into the room, and we all squeezed in close enough to touch one another. I examined the expressionless stare on our new caseworker's face as he listened to the girls' psychologist discuss her conclusions and describe therapy sessions with the girls. Robert was younger than us, short with brown hair cut close, and dark features. He worked in a calm yet perfunctory manner.

"I have already submitted a second letter of assessment documenting their well-being after their brother's death," the psychologist said. "The purposes of our meetings have been to develop rapport, allow the girls the opportunity to express emotion and ask questions, normalize their feelings, and reinforce coping skills as they come to terms with their brother's death. During our first visit, I found Kaylyn to be open and expressive about her understanding of and her feelings surrounding her brother's death and the coping strategies she was using independently and in concert with her family. In our most recent session, she was more hesitant to continue discussing the events at length, though she is working through her grief in other appropriate ways, such as writing about her brother. She has become even more involved in soccer with her friend network, which is an outlet for her." She paused, looking around the room, waiting for questions that were not forthcoming.

"Riley, on the other hand, talked openly about her brother's death and her feelings and discussed the joys of school and friends as a welcome distraction to the focus on her brother's death. She seems to be coping with the tragedy in a manner appropriate to her age and developmental level. You can find more details in my formal letter. I have recommended to Mrs. Seitz that we follow up as needed on whether to bring the girls in for further sessions considering that they seem to be healing in age-appropriate manners and have extensive support systems. I have talked to Mr. and Mrs. Seitz about the nature, progression, and trajectories of children's grief and changes in behavior that may suggest distress and a need for additional support. I will reiterate my advice in the letter, that forcing Kaylyn to continue to discuss the events of that day and her brother's death when she is coping in other ways and has expressed a desire to move on will risk re-traumatizing her further."

Our pediatrician broke in, reiterating the type of care the girls received. "I have no concern for their well-being," she concluded. "These are nothing but responsible and loving parents. Lindsey told me about her history of manic depression voluntarily, and I have never had any concern about her ability to parent her children. I would never have known she suffered from a mental illness unless she had told me."

The pediatrician paused after her conclusion, waiting for a discussion to arise. None did. I gesticulated toward the psychologist, directing my question back at Robert, "So you've heard there is nothing useful that could come out of further interviews of the girls. Why are we really here?"

He leaned in, blank stare undisturbed. "We understand that your children are happy and well-adjusted, but that's not the only issue. We need to find out what happened that day. If there are things they saw or remember."

"So you want to re-traumatize them by asking them details about that day to gather evidence?" I inquired.

The girls' representative in the DCF investigation, Laura, broke in. "And to make sure there is no risk of that happening in the future.

Listen, we all want to hear what Kyle has to say. We've heard your voice loud and clear, but we need to hear his voice. What does he think? How does he feel?"

"No, you don't want to hear his voice. Anything he says or does will be used against him. You get he has been going through an intense trauma since this happened, right? He could barely function, let alone talk to you all."

Exasperated, we ended the meeting. There was nowhere to go, nowhere to run, only a faint realization that this may not end with my husband alive or our marriage surviving.

55

Riley stood before me with a devious smirk, glancing furtively behind her at my parents who were sitting on the couch. The sunlight burst through the window and placed a glittery haze over their faces, keeping me from deciphering her intent in their expressions. Kyle sat beside me with the same confusion. Her spirit seemed to be caught in time, captured and framed right in front of us. Her spirit exuded the energy that had forced me to put one foot in front of the other since the day of Ben's death.

"Mommy, Mommy! I want to show you something!" she said, jumping up and down as if she were attached to a spring.

"Extraordinary!" she screamed, as she and my parents immediately placed their index finger in the air next to their faces. "My teacher told us you have to put your finger up when you hear someone say a big word. The word is extraordinary! And extraordinar*ily* gets two fingers!" Her jubilant cackles filled the room as she lay down on the floor on her back, kicking her gangly legs in the air. Kaylyn looked up inquisitively from where she was playing with Legos in the corner of the room and then smiled. We all laughed.

Despite the ongoing investigations, moments of lightness broke through with ever-increasing frequency, and we began to feel less guilty about it. A smile, a laugh, a joke, a hug. Those glimmers caught me off guard. The reality of the loss of Ben was constant and overwhelming, like a separate, parallel consciousness, but in certain moments, we were finding space for the loss—and the hope.

The breeze of a crisp New England fall hit our faces as the girls and I screeched the words of our favorite country song out the window, swaying to the rhythm... Riley turned the knob on her pink stereo, grabbing my hand to dance in our sunroom as Kyle cooked dinner in the kitchen... I became a normal soccer mom for a moment, smiling and cheering as I watched Kaylyn engrossed in the pure joy of the game on Sundays, fresh carpet of green beneath our feet and a tapestry of fall leaves above our heads.

The other moments would always be there. I looked up from my coffee at Tazza and time stopped. *If only*, I thought. However, I was learning to allow those moments to wash over me as I turned to focus on my still-existing children engrossed in their books, sipping mango-strawberry smoothies across from me.

Early on, these moments just confused me. Was I allowed to smile? To laugh? What if I wasn't miserable all the time or realized I hadn't cried yet one day? A friend had told me that when I was not on my knees, it was because Ben lived in me here *and* in Heaven above. I began to think she could possibly be right. My family was right in front of me, and Ben would want us to continue to live and be happy.

One afternoon, I caught myself in one of those joyful moments as I drove Kaylyn home from soccer, and as the guilt seeped in, I turned to her.

"Can I tell you something? After Ben's death, I'm sad and it's very painful. Every day. But, you know, I'm happy too, especially in the moments with you girls. Getting up in the morning, reading, writing, being with you and Daddy and friends. Can I say that? Is it okay?"

"Yes, Mom," she replied, "of course."

That night, after homework and dinner, the girls begged me for dessert, and after the many days of screaming, crying, disbelief, and anger, I found myself spraying a gob of whipped cream into their mouths, and then my own, listening to the laughter resonate within our house. We had found joy in a simple moment.

56

July 5, 2014

"I'll race you," Kyle said and turned to me with a mischievous glint in his eyes.

"You don't want to race me," I retorted, challenging him. "Loser has to do twenty push-ups in the sand."

"You're on," he said, laughing.

It was our last Saturday together before Ben died. We dug our toes into the sand behind an invisible starting line, pushing each other and scrambling for the best position. Friends began to line up behind us to watch. The girls played off to the side, having moved on from swimming as the sun disappeared beneath the horizon. Ben was sound asleep in his bed at home, after having had a playdate with my parents. Cheers began to erupt. "On your mark, get set," someone yelled, "go!"

We were off. To the volleyball net and back. The darkness hid the natural divots of the sand, deep and pliable. I slipped as the sand turned beneath my right foot, and he surged ahead.

"I win!" he gesticulated with his hands in the air as he crossed the finish line.

I feel like a kid again, I thought, as I leaned over, breathing hard and laughing.

The girls' friends circled around me, counting off my push-ups. "You can't do twenty," someone yelled. They were right. I chuckled. Later that night, I sat in his lap on the picnic bench, watching the girls roast s'mores at the bonfire with their friends. *We have a good life,* I thought. We are finally happy.

We just simply fit. Our sarcasm and silliness but also in some deeper way, as if he was the only one who could be there for me in my darkest hours to save me. We had known from first sight that we were meant to be together and always would be. It was a give and take. While I drudged through law school and long hours at the office, I returned home to steaming plates placed neatly on the table, kids happily eating and giggling with their father, and an empty seat waiting for me. He had agreed to be a stay-at-home father when we moved to Connecticut for my job, and he would have it no other way. He cherished the time with his children, a time I did not get. Kaylyn often reminisced about her preschool years in the neighboring town, daddy-daughter dates at Starbucks while Riley was in her morning class, drawing pictures on any scrap of paper they could find, playing games together on his phone. Long walks in the park in the afternoon, Kyle helping them across the monkey bars at the playground. Kaylyn wanted to rewind time, as did we.

When Ben was born, the girls were school age, so Kyle had the days alone with just him and his son. I often felt jealous of the bond they forged through such intimate interactions, oftentimes wishing our roles were reversed. When he returned to work, we began sharing the household duties more equally. Ben naturally became a daddy's boy, and the girls became appendages of me. We had fallen in love with more than each other. We had fallen in love with our life together.

57

A home is a living thing. It soaks up the memories at its seams and becomes them. There, beside the kitchen table, is where Ben stood. It was the Saturday before he died. He pointed at his food on the table, turning his head to me, saying "Mama" for the first time. I wrapped one arm around his belly, the other beneath his bottom, lifting him up into his cloth seat attached to the table. His tiny fingers grabbing the fruit, shoving it into his mouth with a smile. There, in the sunroom, where the indoor basketball hoop still stands. That is where Ben rolled a half dozen balls, cordoning them in with his arms. Where Kyle picked him up, allowing him to place the soft, orange basketball into the net with a loud squeal. Again, again, his laughter spoke.

I felt the weight of Ben and his memories in the air, like the heavy humidity on those silent Southern nights of my childhood, as if I could physically feel them, cut through them with my arms. They engulfed me; they were around every corner. I wanted to wrap my body around them and run from them all at the same time. Instead, we stood motionless in time, unable to move forward, forever looking back.

I often remembered one of the first nights we spent in our house after Ben died. The memories had come like electric shocks to my body. Kyle leaned over the sink in our bathroom washing his face as I stood to the side deep in thought.

"You stood right here! Don't you remember?" I prodded, walking over behind him and stomping my feet onto the floor in recognition.

He paused washing his face and looked at me in the mirror, worried.

"You had just gotten him out of bed. He was on your hip." I pictured his ruffled hair, sleepy eyes, green alligator pajamas. "Remember? He was right here. Now he's gone."

"Yes, I remember." He dried his face with a towel to avoid my penetrating stare.

"Agh!" I turned, pounding my fist into the wall. I crumpled in pain, holding my hand. Nothing he could say would make the pain go away. It had to fester for the moment.

Over time the house released its tight grip on our bodies, as if it molded to our internal stages of grief. The acute stage of denial, isolation, and anger giving way to depression and a general malaise. The comforting desire to hold him again through the memories carried in the bones of our house, emerging from the intense pain engendered in the earlier stages. I felt my mind torn between the need to shed the skin of the past with an intense desire to wallow in its depth, to keep it alive. The house, our town had seeped through our pores unnoticed until we were inseparable. Even the pockmarks that had appeared were now part of us. The parking spot where Kyle had parked for coffee that morning, the street leading to his office. For each blight, there was a complementary reminiscence of our life together. The park where we had played, the streets where Ben had once walked. We knew we may have to move far away from our town in order to heal and build anew, but there was a magnetism to our life that was. A move would be an embittered laceration. A hesitant goodbye to the life we had built. Of beautiful New England falls, auburn and golden leaves swirling in the crisp air, picnics at Kent Falls, pumpkin and Christmas tree farms, and swirling, majestic snow. But it was time for a fresh start.

58

Part of his spirit remained in his room. I felt it ooze around my body and mold itself to my form as I shut the door for privacy. I held a camera in my hand, along with the boxes. I had to capture the essence of him still held in his possessions before placing them gently into a reservoir of the past. I felt possessive of my son and his belongings, as if his death had fractured his lineage, leaving only me as a parent. Only me who could say a proper goodbye. The process was personal and private.

His white crib pushed up against the wall closest to the door. Sheets speckled with aqua turtles and fish, still crumpled from his last night's sleep. My hands did not reach to straighten them, my eyes were fixated on the outline of his body on the mattress. A wrinkle in time. The rocking chair by the window. I had plopped down on its plaid cushion when I went into labor, frantically calling my doctor. The cotton fibers still retained the energy of my excitement. The fulsome power of creation and birth. Toys thrown into a pile in his gray pack-n-play, having been hastily collected around the house by my parents after his death. I leaned over at the waist, burying my face in the cushion of his changing pillow to muffle the screams.

With the pain expunged, I got to work. Creating labels of "Ben's clothes," "Ben's toys," and the simple "Ben's memories" before carefully placing the physical remnants of my son into the corresponding boxes. With the cleansing completed, I closed the door and walked away, leaving a part of myself behind. Strangers would now walk across his floor while viewing our house. Ben was no longer there; it was only a room.

59

I had been searching for a home as long as I had been searching for myself, which led me to wonder whether a home was more than a physical repository of memories. Whether it was more of a space that existed within, something that was part of us. A space that we could always fall into when nothing else was left. I did know it was more than the plywood and cement beneath my feet, and I had not found that space yet in my life. I had run from one home to the next, but they always felt like foreign bodies, as if I was trying on another person's coat. Too tight, too loose, not quite right.

When I arrived with the girls in Colorado in September, two months after Ben's death, I found myself searching for another new home, but this time not just to escape myself, to escape the world. House hunting, a new city where no one knew us. Anonymity, no abrasive memories greeting us at every turn. The last home the realtor showed us held the energy of the sun. An old-world, Tuscan-style house, with textured walls of gold. A lightness was there, and space, a yard in which to play. It sat in the foothills overlooking the city, with views of Garden of the Gods. We felt as if we could fly… and maybe we could.

The remainder of our two-day trip was spent sightseeing again. We needed to make sure it felt right, but most importantly, we needed to find hope. A rope out of the dark pit of despair. Our hike together, mother and daughters, in Garden of the Gods carried with it a sparkling energy. The sun was blinding, not a cloud in the sky. I felt a sense of freedom as we ran and laughed along the trail, and the reality of our life slipped away if just for the day. The girls posed atop our favorite outcropping, and I snapped pictures. That day, that location, those emotions. It felt like home, as if I had fallen into myself. Into Ben. Weeks later, as I showed the photographs to a friend, she paused, zoomed in, then zoomed in some more. "Look, do you see that?" As I bent over my computer screen, I did see it. In a picture taken from the outcropping, across the valley toward Pikes Peak. Right in front of us, a tiny spiral of blue energy floating endlessly to the sky.

60

We sat together in her kitchen eating gorgonzola cheese and homemade pastries with apricot jam, sipping a glass of wine. Night had fallen, only the static of her baby monitor broke through the silence. I had not known Amy before our tragedy. Amanda, a mutual friend, had introduced us in September at school pick-up. It felt odd, and I wondered if I had been relegated to being a spectacle for the rest of my life. A few weeks later she planned a dinner with the three of us, and then I realized there had been a reason for our introduction.

"I need to tell you something." She sat across from me at her kitchen island, and I looked at her questioningly. "Sometimes I have dreams or see things. I've always been like that." She paused, most likely waiting for me to laugh and walk out the door, but I remained seated.

"Around July eleventh, I had a dream. But it wasn't really a dream. I sat straight up in bed and he was right before my eyes. It was a blond-haired boy. I knew it wasn't my son, so I just overlooked it like people normally do with dreams, assuming it was one of his friends I had seen before."

"Okay," I was waiting for the punchline.

"It was before they had released pictures of Ben. They had only released your names, so I had never seen him before. Then later in the month when you were on television and they ran a picture of Ben... I realized the boy in my dream was Ben. I almost physically vomited and called Amanda to tell her."

I let a breath escape, not quite knowing what to make of her story yet. I had never truly thought about any theories of consciousness or dreams. I took life after death as a given but had no idea what it really meant. I had been taught Ben was in Heaven, and that was the end of it.

"About a month later, I went to reiki. Do you know what that is?"

"Nope," I responded.

"Your body has energy fields. Reiki is the art of healing by working with your body's own energy. I'd seen her once before. Christine has an office off the beaten path. She doesn't advertise and only works through word of mouth. I'd heard of her from a friend. During my first session, she told me a man was there, who had passed away. He wanted me to know he had fallen but was fine now, and most importantly, he wanted his wife to know he liked what she had done to her engagement ring."

My instinct turned into consternation.

"Here's the thing. One of my male friends had died in 9-11. He was in the Twin Towers. I waited for a long time and then finally called his wife. She told me she had turned her engagement ring into a necklace, which she never takes off."

I was not sure whether I believed any of her story, but if it was true, it gave me a sense of hope.

"So during my second visit a few weeks ago, she was working on my body on the table. She told me she saw a little boy with blond hair, running around in a circle playing with a woman standing off to the side. He kept playing with his mouth, like he was trying to send a message. She asked me if I had a son who had died. I told her, 'No, not unless there is something I didn't know. I just saw him thirty minutes ago!'" We both chuckled. "She told me the boy was happy and playing. He just wanted us to know he was okay." She looked up at me with an anticipatory glance.

"Is that even possible?" I asked. I didn't know enough to try to believe a story like that, despite my desire to find it true.

"I don't know. But it happened. Did Ben play with his mouth?"

"No, but when Kyle rocked him, he would reach up and finger his lips. It was hard for him to settle otherwise. He did it every night."

"It wasn't just Christine either, Lindsey. A few weeks later, I was having coffee with someone in town. A friend of hers walked in, and they started talking. Apparently, she can sense things too. She turned to me, telling me she hoped I didn't think her odd, but that she saw a blond-haired boy running around in a circle playing beside me. Just like during reiki."

I looked out the window into the darkness. This was all too much for me to process. "Maybe one day I will go see Christine. Can you give me her number?" I asked. I would keep it, just in case.

61

An energetic peace overcame me when I walked into Christine's small office on October 16, three months after Ben's passing. The smell of lavender, candles glowing on wooden shelves, Buddhist symbols lying about. She sat me down at a small desk against the far wall, the long reiki table behind her back, a small lamp lit the room in the corner. She had a lightness in her presence and a gentleness as she spoke.

"So how did you find out about me?" she asked.

"My friend, Amy, recommended that I come see you."

"You know I can do things other than reiki. Correct? I can sense things. Are you open to that too or just reiki?" she inquired.

"I'm open to whatever." I was hesitant, tentative, unbelieving through my strong roots in organized religion.

Almost as a relief, her body seemed to release tension. "Good, because there's so much chatter and energy in here, I'm already getting a headache." She laughed.

"Okay," I responded slowly, still uncertain. She opened up a notebook and grabbed a pen to write as we progressed during the session.

I examined her calm presence. She had sandy blonde hair that flowed in waves past her shoulders. She was only a few years older than me but had an air of wisdom beyond her years. She closed her blue eyes and explained that she would take a few deep cleansing breaths before we got started. As she did this, I felt myself breathing deeply with her. Relaxing into the moment. Allowing myself to be present.

"I don't know where to start," she said, perplexed. There's a lot going on with you right now, so many different directions. I just don't know what all this means yet." She began scribbling on the pad of paper in front of her. A circle with arrows shooting off in different directions.

"'Respect,' you need to personally heal from within before you can branch out, and 'quiet,' I'm getting the word quiet. There is a wedding ring, issues with your marriage."

I sat quietly, allowing her to speak freely.

"All this chaos isn't meant for you." She paused, looking up.

She continued, speaking rapidly, "You need to Respect yourself, find the Quiet. To do what you are really supposed to do, you need to take care of yourself or you will break down."

Yes, I'm headed in that direction, I thought.

"Also, the word 'faith' is really important. Have you had a shift in faith or religion recently?"

"Yes, in a way. I grew up in a Southern Baptist household. True 'in-the-box' religion. I've had some experiences recently where I'm beginning to question whether there is more to reality and God than that."

"Right, well you need to broaden your view of religion into the more spiritual side. Also, I'm getting the letter 'B.' Who is that?"

My breathing stopped as tears rushed to my eyes. "Benjamin."

"Woah," she chuckled, "it just got silent. The chatter in the room just went away. Who is Benjamin?"

"My son."

"He has passed?"

"Yes, he has."

She sat back in her chair, looking at me and released a deep breath. "Oh my, I'm so sorry. I can't imagine." She returned to her sketch pad. "He's blond. I see him playing around in a circle, laughing. There is a woman in the background. She doesn't look old. He's playing with his mouth." She looked up before continuing. "Benjamin. He is linked to Faith somehow." She wrote the word "faith" on her pad, with an arrow pointing to the larger circle.

"He is saying 'Mama. Isn't she wonderful?' He is playing with your hair." There is a longing in her voice. "A lot of light just came into the room, too. He's saying, 'I'm okay, see?' I'm getting a lot of energy and vibrations."

She looked at me deeply. "'You are beautiful. You are wonderful.' That's what he's saying. Now you understand it's not like he is really saying this, as we imagine in the physical world. I have to put it into words. He is crawling all over your husband, kissing him, saying, 'I love you. It's okay.'"

I shook my head, tears forming again.

"I'm worried about who is taking care of him," I prodded her.

"He says not to worry. I feel many are there with him. I feel one woman in particular." She paused.

"Kyle's mother passed away when he was young," I inserted, shaking my head.

"He says he just went to sleep. I see him sitting up but slightly reclined, looking out a window. He cried at first because he was alone, but then he just went to sleep." She stopped. "Does this make any sense?"

I nodded, tears flowing, asking her to continue. "He woke up and thought it was the sun, but it was a beautiful light. He wanted to touch it, but then it became him. He was light." She was talking as a child would. 'It was so cool!' That's what he is saying. Then he just went into the light."

"Listen, don't worry about who he is with. The Divine came to get him. He wasn't meant to be here. It's not about you but him. His vibrations." She paused, as if listening. "They are so strong. He had another purpose."

I could not stop my tears at this point, and I told her who I was.

"Oh my," she said as she leaned back in her seat again. "I'm so, so sorry. I heard about that but I don't watch the news. I had no idea. I'm so very sorry."

She placed her hands on the table, looking into my eyes. "As traumatic as it was, he was here to put a higher purpose in motion. It's all linked to Faith somehow, expanding, vibrations, energy."

She scribbled the word "see" beneath her other sketches. "You need to open your eyes and *see*. He is leading you to who you are. You just need to allow yourself to be."

I needed to just Be, so very desperately, but I could not fathom how Ben could lead me there. After the first part of the session, she asked me to lie down on the table as she ran her hands lengthwise, inches above my body. I felt nothing but sensed she did. I simply existed in the quiet of that moment, thinking of Ben. Her movement appeared as if she were raking the sand off my body, flicking her hands into the air at the end of each swipe as if getting rid of the dust to dust.

62

Something happened inside of me during that reiki session. I felt now that there could be a pathway to Ben, and I needed to learn more. I was determined to try meditation. I understood prayer. I had been taught in my youth that through prayer, I spoke to a human God who would listen and respond with his desires. However, I did not understand meditation, so this would be my first hesitant step outside of the box. It felt illicit, as if I needed to hide my ventures from other Christians, for if they found out, I would surely be branded as a heretic. If I believed in God, prayer was the only way to communicate, but prayer was not working, and my journey back to believing in God was like treading water.

I thought back to the moment of calm in the emergency room. Able to think more clearly, I could add descriptors to the experience. It was as if my mind transcended my body and the walls around me. The physical reality and struggles I had held onto so tightly over my lifetime had fallen away. Could it be that the moment of calm held within it more truth than the four corners of the room within which I had stood?

I had come to believe there might indeed be some power in the mind outside our bodies, so meditation was worth a try. I had found some meditation CDs that were of particular interest to me, which used various frequencies of sound to mimic the electrical activity present in altered states of consciousness—from dream states to out-of-body experiences. My journey to find Ben had turned me into an experimenter. I had the benefit of knowing what it felt like to have no reality, therefore no assumptions as to what was true, and when there was no one truth, there were only infinite possibilities.

On October 26, I decided to attempt my first meditation session. I laid my iPhone and earbuds on the spare bed, closed the door tightly, and turned the fan down on low. I had to build a sanctuary where I could quiet my mind. I had been living with an unquiet mind for so long, the potential for success was not promising. I lay out supine on the bed, placed my hands by my side and turned my headphones up loudly enough to drown out the noises from the living room.

The first sound on the recording was a shock to my system. A deep, bone-bending hum. "Om…" created not by voices but by vibrations, transferred from headphones to eardrums and through my entire upper body. Thoughts still ran rampant through my brain. *My hands are too cold. The television is blaring,* I thought. *Ben's funeral, investigations, the lights are too bright.* I took a deep breath, exhaled, and let my mind float away. I felt connections to thoughts dissolve. I visualized blackness. The blackness my life had become, the void of that night in the emergency room, and a single light. A pinpoint light. I concentrated on the luminescence. *I'll call it my angel,* I thought. *My angel is light.* The darkness slowly tunneled into a smaller hole, a primordial jelly-like consistency with rings of purple, orange, red, and blue, which slowly became the curves of the mouth of an oyster shell and then an entire oyster shell. Then I was one with and inside the oyster, a pearl and the ocean all at once. I was not floating on the surface of the ocean or swimming in it; I *was* the ocean. One molecule of the ocean but also the entirety of it. I then flowed through the waves onto a white sandy beach. I felt the sun, crisp and bright. A sense of purity. A palm tree stood in the distance.

Before me, undisturbed by my existence, walked a tall white-winged angel beside another smaller being. I did not feel like it was a person or a spirit who had passed. It was a spirit prior to being, a girl with blonde hair pulled back in a ponytail. She walked looking up at the angel. Ben was not there. I sensed he was in another place. Another realm, if there was such. Then again, I was swimming, yet I was part of the water. I *was* the water, a fish yet breathing. I slowly crawled out of the darkness back to the room, with fan whirring and television in the background. I could not fathom where my mind had taken me, but it was far beyond the room in which I lay. If but for an instant, I had been comforted. A familiar sense of myself, which I had never felt before.

63

The comfort I felt during meditation was a sense of exploration, as if I were liberated from a physical world created by my own mind. I was outside of the mind, understanding through pure experience. More was in that space within me than existed during an entire lifetime.

Having been born in the era of the scientific, like other Americans my age, I had never truly contemplated the concept of an otherworldly or purely spiritual reality. I only had the physical reality before my eyes. Despite my upbringing in the Christian church, I had even seen the belief in God or any higher power lose steam in society over my lifetime. I was witnessing the end result of a process that had begun long before my birth. In the Western world, the rise of the secular materialism of the nineteenth century had ushered in the gradual removal of God from everyday life. Like many others, I understood reality only through the physical or material, the gears churning under the pure force of progress.

This focus on progress was a byproduct of evolution itself, which is centered on control and survival. In the twenty-first century, this meant material control of the world around us, a focus on careers, success, money, to provide for our families. Static. Nonstop movement. Yet when Ben died, it had all fallen away. All of the material and control. Everything. It had not been the core of me as I had once thought. It left me only with a feeling of emptiness. Ben was gone, not in the physical arena anymore, and I was left searching. I had religion to rely upon, but it failed me too, or at least my limited view of it. My scientifically trained brain was not even sure it was possible for God, or a purely spiritual world, to exist, and with my son dead, I could not have faith in an impossibility.

Because of the static and rush of life, I rarely felt anything other than the daily goings-on of material existence. I sat in church some Sundays but did not feel the intense energy and harmony of my youth. The emotions running through my body until tears formed. The excitement. It fell flat. What had I felt as a child, in the small country church, skipping down the steps simply enjoying the organ music emanating from inside and the breeze on my bare legs? I wanted to feel that again.

Philosopher of religion, Rudolf Otto, posits that this sense of the "numinous," or something beyond our physical reality, is the basis of all religion.[12] Religion, like science, became a language of reality. Ralph Waldo Emerson, an American Transcendentalist, often described the feeling of the numinous in nature, when humans were removed from the static of everyday life. "Crossing a bare common, in snow puddles, at twilight, under a clouded sky, without having in my thoughts any occurrence of special good fortune, I have enjoyed a perfect exhilaration. I am glad to the brink of fear."[13] The moment I stood in the sunlight at Garden of the Gods. Walking through the woods on a crisp autumn day. The birth of a child, looking into his eyes. Being taken away by the rise and fall of a symphony. The calm. Yet those moments of the numinous were few and far between for me.

Meditation had been different for me though, which gave me hope. I had never questioned the assumption that my brain created consciousness. Of course, it did. I had thoughts and emotions, likes and dislikes, memories. I knew consciousness was not related to my soul, for the soul was something ephemeral, ineffable, nothing related to real life or my mind. I expected modern science to support my assumptions. However, I found that it was proving anything but the supreme reign of the physical over the spiritual. For example, research has supported the transmission or filter model in which consciousness comes from somewhere outside the brain and is mediated or filtered through it. What results is an awareness limited by our physical bodies, our senses and neurons. We cannot *know* reality unless we transcend these limitations.

The notion is not new, that a reality exists beyond the physical world we experience on a daily basis, filtered through our brains. As with Plato's Allegory of the Cave, man sees only shadows cast by real objects illuminated outside his world, mistaking them for reality. He is imprisoned in his own mind.[14] Philosophers and mystics have long described the existence of a reality beyond the senses, beyond concepts and words. In Hinduism, it is referred to as *maya*, an illusion created by our senses that masks an ultimate reality. Several ancient Jewish and Christian theologians espoused this view as well, of the soul trapped in the physical, with a true reality out there (or within ourselves). A reality beyond conception, only to be known when the limitations of our intellect are transcended.

I had been raised to have faith in a higher reality, in God, but what if I could experience it myself in real life on more than just a fleeting basis? What if I could experience something that I may never understand but only feel? On an ordinary day, through prayer or meditation. I had gotten a taste of it, and it was a sweet relief.

Meditation has long served a distinct purpose for Eastern religions. It is a method of quieting the mind, reducing the static created by the illusion of our daily lives, to allow the mind to transcend. To become aware of what truly is. In Hinduism, it is a conduit for our individual consciousness to unite with the universal consciousness, or Brahman. In Buddhism, it is a method of transcending the finite self into our core, which will ultimately be extinguished. Prayer, much like meditation, is the Christian avenue of connecting to God. Aldous Huxley's description of perennial philosophy views the basis of all religions as the concept that consciousness is the fundamental building block of the universe.[15] It is not limited to Buddhism or Hinduism, it is all-encompassing. It is the sense of the numinous itself, the avenue through which we connect to our higher spiritual selves.

In the words of Sogyal Rinpoche, author of *The Tibetan Book of Living and Dying*, "At the heart of all religions is the certainty that there is a fundamental truth, and that this life is a sacred opportunity to evolve and realize it."[16] However, I did not feel as if I was evolving. I was stagnant, mired down in a world not of my making and I was far from knowing my true self, or God for that matter, but during the calm in the emergency room, something had existed. I was just not sure what that something was. It was not empty; it was consummate fullness. It was a comfort, a sense that no matter how horrible the circumstances were in that moment, they were just as they were supposed to be. All was well. It was some form of consciousness and understanding beyond my body, beyond physical reality itself.

Rinpoche describes a scenario whereby a man walks into his home to find out he has been robbed. Through shock and despair, as his mind tries to reconstruct all that he has lost, the man realizes he has lost everything. The agitation and shock subside as a "sudden, deep stillness enters, almost an experience of bliss, no more struggle, no more effort, because both are hopeless."[17] The man must give up. He has no choice. His mind is freed and is able to rest in a deep state of peace, glimpsing the deathless nature of the enlightened mind.

I couldn't help but wonder. *Had that been the calm?*

64

When Kyle and I walked into the small apartment in the Upper West Side of Manhattan, I wanted to see how far my mind could travel. I had first heard of Alexandre Tannous through a recent conference on meditation and consciousness in New Bedford, Massachusetts. He had been noted in Eben Alexander's *The Map of Heaven* as the ethnomusicologist and sound therapist who had taken Dr. Alexander back to the realms he had crossed during his near death experience.[18] I held hopes he could guide me closer to Ben.

Books lined the shelves on each side of the entryway. Large gongs and smaller instruments were set up on the wall in his living room next to a small stereo system. He introduced himself by shaking our hands with an excited fervor. He was dressed in stone-washed jeans, a t-shirt, and sandals, with brown curls falling into his face. I needed someone on the cutting edge of research, and I got the immediate sense he was just scholarly yet innovative enough to meet my needs. He guided us into the living room to sit on a plush couch as he spread two bear skin rugs on the floor between the couch and instruments. He began by explaining the science behind his approach, grabbing an instrument and bringing it over to me.

"This is a Himalayan singing bowl. I've traveled around the world to find these ancient instruments: Nepal, Tibet, India, the Peruvian Amazon. They are made of bronze, an alloy of tin and copper," he explained, allowing me to run my fingers across its edges. "I use these in sound healing and to induce altered states during meditation. I use what are called harmonic overtones. See, feel these vibrations." He tapped the bowl gently with a wooden stick and swirled it around my head. I felt the vibrations wash over me, carried through the air to unite with my body. He then touched the bowl to the skin of my arm. It was electric. I was finally moved—not only emotionally, but deeper—somewhere inside of myself.

He guided us to lie down beside each other on the bear skin rugs and to close our eyes. I heard his footsteps and squeaking floorboards, the clank of instruments as he gathered his symphony for us. He began with gongs, and I felt a current of air as he walked around our bodies, moving the gong over, around, and across just inches from our skin. I could have been flying. "Focus on the sound of the overtones. Let your mind fall away," he instructed us.

At first my brain clamped hold of the noises surrounding me, doors slamming in the hallway, floorboards squeaking, a gentle clearing of the throat. Then as the minutes passed, I felt my body grow heavy, as if it were falling into the wooden floor itself, weighted down by my muscles and bones. Then I felt a sense of something effervescent leaving, traveling ever so slowly up my body and out into the air through my scalp. I welcomed the freedom of letting it go. In doing so, a vision came into my mind. I was lying supine on the bear skin rug with streams of smoke floating up from my body.

He then moved on to chimes. I had expected to see scenes or visualize shapes like I had in my first meditation session in our home, but nothing materialized. I allowed my body to remain heavy, my mind as light as the clouds. I heard the sound of a shruti box, moving back to gongs, deep and penetrating. I then found myself tumbling in a darkness, similar to space, as if I was rolled up in a blanket. I saw a blue shape, an endless knot levitating in the distance. Ben's face floated by in a flash, here and then gone. I had not been expecting to see him, so I fought it at first.

When I could regain my bearings, I let him in. His pull was magnetic. I could touch his skin, but not with my hands, with my mind. I gently pushed his hair out of his face. We then became one, connected and true. I felt him within my heart. He *was* my heart. It was all-encompassing, complete unconditional love. I (or we) began flying through the darkness. I saw the shape of a caterpillar and then a dove, which merged into an essence of golden structures. They appeared like mountains of golden treasures but not any geographic structure I had seen on Earth. They were otherworldly. I then saw a rose with thorns, a teddy bear, and a conductor's hat. Then the comfort and sense of love began to recede as I felt Ben leaving me.

I asked him to stay.

I'm here with you all the time, he said as he showed me a picture of a ladybug.

I just have to go for now. He glanced off into the distance. Then grinned.

Look mommy! I'm as big as the sun and as small as the head of a pin. Silence.

I love teddy bears!

I asked him to show me more, but he did not want to.

I just want you to hold me, he said.

So we again became one, tumbling through space, as I saw a spinning planet in the distance. After what seemed like an eternity, I felt his presence further and further away from me. The sound of a rain stick, the crack of floorboards, slamming doors in the hallway, honk of car horns.

"Take a few minutes to ground yourself. Breathe and relax," he guided us further into reality. I sat up on the rug, propping myself up with my hands. I was embarrassed by the tear marks already staining my face. Alexandre sat down on the couch across from me, looking at me inquiringly.

"You went really deep, didn't you?" he asked. "You were crying during the meditation. Do you want to tell me what you experienced?"

I wiped my face. "No, I really can't talk about it right now." He nodded in understanding.

65

"It seems that you've connected to your son's spirit," Alexandre later explained. But what did that even mean? My experience in that New York City apartment had been so profound and otherworldly that I had to understand it. I had been raised to believe there were individual souls, housed in our bodies for a lifetime, which through good acts could be returned to a spiritual realm in Heaven. There was no gray area in between, no merging of one soul into the next and especially not conscious communication while still on Earth. The soul was an abstract concept to me, and it had no import in the world of physical reality, yet I had experienced something different that day. I had been inside but outside my physical body. I had been in my mind, but in my soul as well, and most importantly, I had a multisensory interaction with my son, who was not in this physical world, and I needed to understand how that was even possible.

Nada Brahma in classical Sanskrit of India translates to English as "the world is sound" or, according to Joachim-Ernst Berendt, interpreted to mean the world "… vibrates in harmonic proportions."[19] The universe is a vibration. Vibrations are energy. Even matter is energy, for the smallest of particles are in fact waves of probability, existing in limbo, neither here nor there, a fog of uncertainty, until observed by human consciousness. It pins them down. They commit, and we become part of that reality. String theory even posits that the most fundamental particle of the universe is just that—a string—vibrating in discrete harmonic proportions. Various subatomic particles that make up our world may just be different vibrations of that one fundamental string. So were we indeed riding the waves of the universe?

Two particles that were once one remain connected across space and time, forever. They are entangled. Lack of local proximity does not limit their ability to reach one another across the earth and universe. They react to the world in tandem. What affects one affects the other. The world is united, connected. The interconnectedness that is the center of Buddhism. We are one.

During meditation with Alexandre, my consciousness had escaped in cloud-like streams from my body. My mind had danced with Ben. Had our souls touched? Was my mind my soul? And were we both entangled in space, part of something greater, a universal consciousness? Something beyond words and concepts? Were we part of God? Possibly my sense in Colorado had been right and Ben was not just in the ground. He was everywhere. He was in a place that we use the word Heaven to describe, and if I could connect with him on Earth, I would be able to connect with him and know him in death.

The vision I had experienced, of wisps of consciousness floating from my body into the air, seemed to mimic the concept of nonlocality now arising within the physics community. With evidence of entanglement, the concept of nonlocality was born. Characteristics of particles are correlated across large distances; one particle communicates with the other, and faster than could be attributed to typical transmission methods like light or sound. There exists some nonlocal connection, a nonlocal space, and human consciousness is integrally involved. We form a holistic system.

Just what nonlocality means, though, is still up for debate. Some theorists see nonlocal space as comprising additional dimensions. Similarly, string theory actually requires the existence of additional dimensions that are beyond our senses in this three-dimensional world. It has been shown that waves encode information, and information is consciousness. So are our minds integrally connected with the world itself, and to such an extent that we all merge together as one? The sense of the numinous, of God, of love, compassion, and interconnectedness. I was beginning to understand that the spiritual and physical were not mutually exclusive. I could discuss both in the same breath for the first time. I did not have to believe in one or the other—religious or scientific. The physical was indeed supporting the spiritual, even certain concepts born out of Christianity.

The Buddhist metaphor of the universe, Indra's net, describes the universe as a net stretching out infinitely with glittering jewels interwoven and hung at each eye of the net. Looking closely, one will discover that on the polished surface, all of the other jewels in the net are reflected, infinite in number, which also reflect all other jewels. The universe is an interwoven tapestry of brilliant light. It is a sea of interdependence.[20] Thinking back to my meditative state with Alexandre, I felt as if I had existed there, on the surface of a jewel, as if my soul had ridden the vibrations of sound into another realm, where it merged with them, swimming in a sea of thought and life. A world with infinite possibilities and other souls dancing too, in other dimensions beyond the four walls of his apartment. That my mind created and was my world, and we touched God as well. He was the ocean in which we swam, as ourselves, yet as one.

66

I felt like a rat in a test cage spinning endlessly on an exercise wheel. Part of some sort of horrid experiment. The smell of the old courthouse escaped from the wooden walls that seemed to be closing in around me. I was standing in a small enclosed foyer to the side of the courthouse as Peter and I consulted after the status conference with DCF. I had told him I would not divorce Kyle, but I would try to take full custody of the children for now and move with them to Colorado. Kyle could stay in Connecticut until the legal investigation had reached a conclusion. We both hoped this would allay most of their concerns that were at the center of our battle.

I had been examining his face as he spoke, a combination of frustration and helplessness, so I knew what he was going to say before the words escaped. He informed me he had proposed the resolution to the AAG, but she was still pushing back. They would not budge on the other conditions—the interviews with the girls, full release of my medical records, and other consents.

"Then this is not a negotiation really," I responded, dumbfounded. "We are past anything rational and reasonable, aren't we?" I had finally given up hope. The twelve-page social study the caseworker had to prepare under law had come back concluding that our only family weakness was the trauma of losing a family member. We had strong support systems, were a close family, grieving appropriately, all engaged in our own treatment, and the children's emotional, physical, and medical needs were being met. Yet we were still in the midst of a relentless battle with DCF's recommendation at the conclusion of the social study asking for a court-ordered, six-month period of protective supervision.

He told me the group was shocked to learn I wanted to move before the holidays. Laura adamantly opposed the move, saying it would tear the girls apart since their father meant so much to them. Peter had reminded them that the safety plan still did not even allow for Kyle to have unsupervised visits with his children. The AAG appeared shocked. Peter told them that the state had pushed for me to take the kids, asking them what they really wanted at this point. His question was met with silence.

Peter looked up at me. "Lindsey, the AAG threatened to force a state psych evaluation on you both if you don't give in."

My body tightened and blood pressure rose as my will hardened further. We agreed to show good faith in our desire to compromise by signing full releases for my therapist and our daughters' psychologist.

"But they won't get my girls or my psychiatric records," I reiterated to him as we walked into the hall to sign papers. "I will fight to the end for those."

67

I heard the cadence of clanging metal as the rain splattered on the standing puddles in the parking lot. Michele and I ran out of the movie theater with the kids by our side. "Ahhh!" her son screamed with glee, racing ahead to the shelter of the car. "Hey, Kaylyn," he yelled behind as he opened his door, "come over to our house for a playdate?"

Michele nodded to me as she strode after him. "Yes, we'll see you later," she confirmed.

I buckled my girls in, rain soaking my clothes, and jumped into our car, slamming the door behind me. I was dreading the conversation that would ensue.

"Can I go over to their house to play?" Kaylyn asked as we drove out of the parking lot, squirming in her seat with excitement.

"Not today. I'm sorry," I said firmly, trying to stem the tide of our dialogue before it got rolling.

"Why?" she pleaded, her lips quivering.

"Kaylyn," I paused, "you know why. We have to meet with the social worker at 5 p.m. again."

"Nooooo!" She could not contain herself as the tears flowed like the rain against the car window. "I just want to play, Mom!"

"Listen, you know we have to do this since Ben died. It's almost over."

Her words were overtaken by the sounds of sobbing, her face wrinkled like a little pug. "Why do I have to keep talking to people?

Why can't we just go back to the way we were before?" She took a deep breath, as if collecting something important. "I just want to be happy!"

My heart sank with her words, for I had no adequate answer. I was her mother, and I was helpless.

"Things will get back to normal soon, honey, I promise. I'm trying. You just have to trust me. It's taking some time."

"No, no," she cried as we drove toward home. I would stop at the pediatrician's office on the way home to formally document her deep discontent. We had no other option. It had come to that.[21]

68

In the dream, Ben's body appeared dwarfed in the large hallway, dark wooden wall to the right, metal railing leading down the stairs to the left. He toddled away from me without noticing my presence. It was not our house but held a sense of the familiar. When I picked him up and placed him on my hip, he cried as if he did not want to be restrained. He seemed to have a goal in sight and needed freedom to move. After placing him down beside me, which quieted his cries, I was swept into a basement with brown cardboard boxes lining the walls. I sat on an aluminum folding chair across from Jason. He leaned forward toward me with his elbows on his legs. A discerning look. "Why is he crying?" he asked me. In an instant, we were standing in the same hallway with Ben again. Jason reached to pick him up, and Ben's eyes squinted shut with the power of his wails. "Nothing is wrong with him," I told Jason. You have no right to touch him. Stop. No other dialogue passed between us, only a discordant tension. Dread and exhaustion on my part, and with these emotions, it became clear that the scene was taking place in Michele's house. Ben crawled on his bottom down the stairs and toddled over to the front door, where he stood for a moment silently looking out the glass door. He turned to look up at me, his face solid and strong, tears having long since disappeared. Our eyes met one last time, and I understood. The dream slowly faded away as he stood in the doorway, pointing at something far away in the distance.

*****

Robert was greeted with a sea of corrugated moving chaos when he walked into our house for an announced visit on November 7. We had an offer on our house and a signed lease in Colorado to begin November 15. After much thought and heartache, we had decided that a change was best for the family. I knew the painful memories held within the confines of our town would be too much for Kyle to bear in the long run, and if he was charged, we would have no choice. He could not walk the streets as a criminal. Peter had told me that a change in venue to a more neutral state could not harm us and in fact may help us. With an out-of-state move, DCF could either negotiate a settlement and drop our petition, which was unlikely, alert Colorado child protective services and transfer our file, or fight us to the bitter end. I expected one of the latter two options. I was more torn about our move, but Colorado had brought with it a purity and peace during our visits. I was willing to try.

Robert took a seat across from me at the table in our sunroom. There was consternation in his expression. He had the task of parsing out our intentions. I wanted to keep our discussion to the basics, reassure DCF we were taking the right steps to ensure a seamless transition but not show my hand too soon. I knew the neglect petition restricted me from taking the children out of state while the case was ongoing unless I obtained permission first. This was the reason for opening the discussion early on, to give them a chance to negotiate and settle. The fighting had gone on too long. Peter and I had not discussed what would happen if they did not agree to our move. I purposefully withheld the depth of my resolution from Peter. I did not want to scare him with the prospect of a client taking her children out of state without permission from DCF or the court. I wanted to give everyone a chance to negotiate. I would only take this extreme step if forced.

I had not been able to thoroughly research my rights as a citizen to interstate travel. I only had a hazy memory of short discussions during my constitutional law class in law school. I was not a criminal with parole or probation restrictions. I had no court orders against me. I was still a parent capable of making decisions in the best interest of my children, so I was willing to take a calculated risk. I had a hunch that DCF would have to get a court order to force us to return to the state, and I was willing to push that option. The court system would presumably be more neutral, and I would have a chance to plead our case.

"I'd like to talk about your request to move to Colorado. Can you tell me a little more about how you made that decision?" Robert inquired.

It is not a request, I thought, but held my tongue. I could not allow my emotions to run rampant as I had in the past. "I have friends in Colorado and extended family in the Midwest. We are only in New England due to job choices. I want my family to be able to rebuild after everything that has happened. Our move is a personal decision."

"Do you have employment set up?"

"I'm not worried about that. I can work remotely if I need to," I responded. I had no employment set up. I was taking a leap of faith, but I kept that to myself. I could hear my teeth grinding as he spoke. The invasive questions into the private sphere of our life made my body writhe.

"There are military bases in Colorado. I've looked into treatment options. There are so many outpatient trauma programs and specialists. If Kyle comes with me, we can enroll him in something like that if he needs it."

"To what area are you looking to move?"

"Colorado Springs, that's where we have been visiting."

"Have you researched schools in the area?"

"Yes, we found a house in one of the best districts in the city. I've called the school district to ensure there are places in the elementary schools for the girls." I had tried to cover all of my bases in order to lessen their arguments against our move.

"Have you even spoken to the girls about eventually moving?"

"Yes, we actually sat them down on our back patio a few weeks ago and made s'mores together over our fire pit. We weighed the benefits of staying versus moving. We want this to be a family decision, and they both verbalized excitement about the move. They have even told their friends and teachers."

"How would they react if Kyle can't come with them?"

"It would destroy them."

I did not understand at the time that it would not destroy them, that we were stronger than that. We were ingrained in each other. We were each other's world, vibrating in harmonic proportions.

69

Kyle's arms hung loosely at his side, like a rag doll, his right hand still clutching his cell phone. I had heard it in the sound of his voice as he walked down the hallway toward where I was sitting in the living room. Anxiety and desperation. I examined his face. It was no one I recognized. Not a person. Only skin hanging over bones, wrinkles lining his forehead from months of stress. His eyes were hollow, subsumed by something more than fear. It must have been the emptiness of a human surrender.

"They're going to charge me," he stated simply, "with criminally negligent homicide. It's a misdemeanor. Not a felony. It could be worse."

Electricity shot through my body, along with an odd sense of relief. It was the final dropping of the hatchet. There would be no more waiting and watching it dangle above our bodies. *This is it,* I thought without understanding why the phrase kept popping in and out of my head. *This is the moment. The determinative moment.* Of decisions as sharp as shards of glass. Of jumping off a cliff with no land in sight, only faith. *We have to be strong,* I thought. *No cracks. If there is any weakness, any second of faltering, it is all over.*

"I knew it," I whispered, hugging him. "It will be okay. Just trust me. We can get through this. Stay calm. Okay?"

"They are letting me surrender voluntarily. They are working on the arrest warrant now."

We would later find out there had been a scurry of action when Robert had seen the packed boxes.

My hands began shaking. *It is finally all gone. All of it. Our entire life*, I thought. "I'll be right back," I told him, grabbing my cell phone from the end table and racing up the stairs. I closed the door behind me and slumped down onto the footrest of Ben's rocking chair, dialing feverishly.

"Hey, what's up?" Amanda answered.

"They're going to charge him. Criminally negligent homicide." I felt as if I could not collect the appropriate words. My brain had already begun to shut down again from the stress.

"Oh my God," she gasped.

"Listen, you are one of the most rational people I know. My mind is falling apart and I need to run my thoughts by you to see if they are rational or not. I need you to help me."

"Okay, anything you need."

"The girls are going to go to school Monday, and everyone will know. They could see it on the news. A friend could ask them if their dad is going to jail. The media will be at our doorstep again. DCF will only ratchet up their fight against us."

"Yes, you're right."

"We've got a place in Colorado already. I can keep them away from all this. I need to be able to tell them when the time is right. When they can understand. No child their age could understand this right now." I paused, my mind racing. "So, do I go? Tonight? Do I book the next flight and take them out of here? I need to save them. They have so much potential. This could destroy them."

"What would happen if you do that? Is there a court order keeping you here?"

"No, we have requirements in the petition, but the judge didn't transfer it into a court order. I don't know what would happen, but I can deal with whatever comes. I just need you to tell me what you would do, if this were you?"

I heard a long exhale. "I would go. Go. You've got to go," she concluded, and I had already begun packing the bags.

Later that night, I would drive to friends' houses for unexpected, rushed goodbyes of hugs and tears. None of us knew what was happening. We just knew we had to say goodbye. As I exited their homes, adults and children huddled around playing board games, I felt as if I were saying goodbye to everything I knew. My life was gone in an instant.

70

They looked so peaceful. Comforter pulled up around their chins, hair tousled and falling around their faces, hands relaxed and sprawled across the bed. The sight comforted me when my mind could not. A stark, frightening unknown awaited us, but as I stood by their beds watching them sleep at 4 a.m. on November 8, I felt a gentle calm. As I placed my hand against the slight of their back, rubbing them awake, I knew it was the right decision. *This is what I have to protect,* I thought. The ability to dream in peace. They rubbed their eyes, groggy and sleepy.

"Mom?" Riley asked questioningly. "What time is it?"

"Hey baby. It's early. Four a.m. We have changed our plans a bit. We are leaving this morning for Colorado." I would text our landlord on the way to see if we could get into our house earlier than planned. We would sightsee and explore in the meantime.

"Really?" she inquired as I heard Kaylyn shifting in the top bunk. "Cool!"

"Yeah, and I've already packed your bags. It will be a big, fun adventure!" As I squeezed clothes onto their tiny bodies and brushed their ruffled hair, I felt as if I were saying goodbye to something much deeper than the structure of a house and yard, or even a community we called home. I sensed I was saying goodbye to innocence, to any semblance of certainty in an unknown world. I was leaping into the abyss, hoping to be caught.

"Is Daddy coming?" Kaylyn asked.

"No, he's got to finish up some things here for work before he can join us."

She seemed satisfied.

As Kyle hugged the girls outside the JetBlue® gates at John F. Kennedy Airport, I felt an overwhelming sense of fragility. How delicate the link between two beings can be, the trembling of deep love and compassion, the yearning for touch and safety. There was no certainty he would see his children again. Whether his next year would be behind cold barren bars or in the warmth of sunlight, holding his girls.

"I love you," his voice shook as he spoke, kissing them on their foreheads.

"I love you too!" they both squealed, excited for their new adventure. "See you soon!"

Mine was a more hesitant hug, a blur of emotions between our bodies. Of leaving behind life as I knew it, of love in uncertain times. In that moment, it was hard to love a broken man amid the destruction.

PART THREE

71

When philosophers ponder the question *why is there something rather than nothing?* they are presuming there is an absolute nothingness. I wanted it to be true, for when I hit rock bottom and nothing was left, I could finally justify giving up. However, when we walked into the Marriott in Boulder, Colorado on Saturday afternoon, short on cash after months of paying legal fees and preparing to move, and bone-searingly exhausted, I was not sure I believed there would ever be *a nothing* that was left. I was in free fall waiting to hit solid ground, and no matter how many times I felt as if I had reached it, I only kept falling.

"Your card was declined," the front desk clerk stated, handing it back to me.

A rosy embarrassment crossed my face. "Just wait. Let me call the company," I told her. Tears of exhaustion quickly formed as I turned to face the wall. My mind was a blur. *I just need sleep*, I pleaded to myself. I'm breaking down. I stood to the side, allowing other guests to check in. The girls were sitting in front of the fireplace on top of their suitcases, fumbling around with the straps. Exhausted too. Our account had been locked; our payment was overdue. It could be reset but would take hours to work through the system.

I walked back up to the front desk, collapsing with my elbow on the counter, my face lying in my palm. "They fixed it, but it will take a few hours." My eyes tilted toward the ground, as I was unable to hide the tears anymore. "We are so exhausted. I'm sorry."

"Here," she swiped a room key through the scanner. "Just go ahead up to the room and bring the card down when it's set. Just don't tell anyone I did this. Okay?"

I thanked her profusely. *She will never know who we are or understand how she has just helped a desperate family,* I thought as we caught the elevator to our room. We quickly disrobed, wrestled on our pajamas, and with garments strewn across the floor, collapsed into one queen-size bed together.

72

The hills rose out of the shadows of the town in the west, dusty brown with specks of green spruce and pine. Arctic blue sky, indigo clouds dappling the horizon, heralded the arrival of the first snow of the season. We had awoken to a chilly but sunny Colorado day. The hills beckoned with the promise of isolation. Just us, the whirling wind and the dirt beneath our feet. I felt as if we were alone on a deserted island, the freedom to breathe uninhibited being the only sustenance we needed.

We sat beside the fireplace at a coffee shop, eating pastries and muffins. There had been a release of tension that morning, arising from the sense of physical freedom that we could hold onto. My mind and body needed a respite from the constant fighting, and we had found it here. A child-like energy engulfed our table as the girls sifted through sets of Pokémon cards. I sat with my fingers curled around steaming coffee, jealous of their naiveté.

"Mom, do you want some of my cards?" Kaylyn asked.

"Will they give me special powers?" A rush of excitement spread through my body. In that moment, I wanted to be a child again. I wanted to believe in special powers and magic shields since my mind had already considered what Monday would bring.

"Oh yes, Mom. They will!" she exclaimed.

I picked the shiniest and most colorful card in the pack, which I assumed would carry the most power. To my disappointment, I was wrong, for I was left with Rhyhorn: "strong, but not too bright, this Pokémon can shatter even a skyscraper with its charging tackles." I laughed, telling them thank you and placing the card in my purse. I would carry the card with me for months as a reminder of that morning. A new beginning, a morning of laughter and hope. For an instant I had felt proud as I sat watching my daughters trade cards, giggles resonating across the coffee shop, a glimmer in their eyes. They were safe and at peace, if just for one more day.

73

The next day, we were determined to get a hike in before the snow arrived. I needed to see if we could physically walk out our worries, beat them into submission within the earth. As we sat in the lobby eating breakfast, my phone rang, sending a pulse of anxiety up my spine. *And so it begins*, I thought.

It was Robert, and he sounded anxious and irritated. "I hear you are in Colorado. The school told us the girls weren't in today and wouldn't be returning."

"Wow, that was fast," I retorted. I was beyond my limit of control. "Yes, I've moved a week early. I'm here with the girls."

"Lindsey, there is a court proceeding going on. You can't just leave," he responded. "And you are supposed to give us notice before you leave the state."

"We've already given you notice of our intent to move. Robert, I'm protecting *my*," I said emphasizing the word, "children. An arrest warrant is out for my husband. Do you have any idea what they would face in Connecticut? With the media? At school? This is in their best interests." I was still their mother, which meant something.

"You need to give me the address where you are living."

"No. I'm not at our house yet. I'm in Boulder, and I will not give you the address of where we are temporarily staying." I kept telling myself he did not need to know that unless he was going to send the local child protective services or police to find us. I desperately needed a few more days of peace and would do anything to get it. "I'm protecting my children and I'll give my address to my attorney. Your attorney can now communicate directly with mine instead of you calling me."

"I'll have to consult with our legal department."

The state of constant anxiety that had threaded its fingers through our lives for the past four months was returning. "Okay, girls, let's go hiking!" I tried to rein it in. For this instant, possibly just this day, I was still alone, in control, with my girls.

When we arrived at Chautauqua Park in southwest Boulder, the winds were beginning to pick up, a portent of the incoming storm. Bundled in layers, we marched up the hill on a two-mile hike, stopping along the way for the girls to play. They stood atop a large boulder, hands on hips, legs outstretched like teenagers, grinning. *They are queens of their world today. They are happy,* I reassured myself. As we rounded the bend at the crest of the trail, my phone rang again. It was Rebecca, one of Robert's supervisors. I stood reiterating our previous conversation. I watched the leaves flutter in the distance, a gentle gust blowing through the elms and ashes that were just past peak. There was a beauty in the chilly air, a hope within the tempest turning toward us. "Listen, I've got to go. I'm hiking with my kids," I told her as I hung up the phone. They stopped a few feet from where I stood talking and posed for a photograph, rust colored strokes of God in the background.

74

Kyle was working feverishly on Monday, throwing the remainder of our belongings into the back of the moving truck, when he saw the car pull into our driveway. Movers milled about, haphazardly tossing items into boxes and then placing the boxes into the truck. He was rushed, aware of the length of time it would take to drive our belongings out to us. He was already distraught and on edge, so when the social workers stepped out of the car, his stomach sank with dread. He was not sure how many more confrontations he could take.

He glanced at their faces, which appeared frustrated and angry, and their emotions only escalated as they walked by the side of the moving truck. Kyle guided them to the back porch to talk in private.

"We're here to discuss your wife's relocation to Colorado without our knowledge."

"It was not without your knowledge. We told you we were moving," Kyle responded. "We think it's in the best interests of the girls considering my impending arrest."

"Are you planning on turning yourself in?"

"Of course!" he responded, frustration growing. "My attorney is taking care of all of that. I haven't been hiding. I've been right here. There was an agreement that I would just voluntarily surrender. There isn't going to be a formal arrest." He paused, trying to contain his growing anger. "Do you have any idea how the media attention would affect the girls?" he asked them.

"We need to know your wife's address. We asked her this morning and she wouldn't give it to us. We will be making a call to the Colorado State Child Protective Services and explaining the unresolved neglect petition filed in court here."

"I don't have an exact address right now," he stated, "but I'll provide one as soon as I have it." He knew I was staying in hotels until the house was ready. I had pleaded with him to withhold my location. I needed him to buy us some more time. As a family, we desperately needed a reprieve from the battles being waged in Connecticut.

"How can you not know where they are living?" they said, their voices escalating.

"You know what? I don't even understand why you filed a claim against her."

"It was because she is the mother."

"Yes, she is the mother. That's the point. Your continued involvement is not in the best interests of my children."

Robert would later report that Kyle became increasingly upset and emotional with the conversation about how DCF's continued involvement was having a negative impact on the children. He observed that Kyle was about to cry until he was interrupted by contractors moving his furniture.

As I lay in bed that night, after hearing of their combative repartee, I felt lost and hopeless. I wondered if we even knew what we were fighting about anymore, or why.

*****

The next morning, Kyle experienced the same emotions I had the night before, sitting in the six-by-four cell waiting to be photographed and fingerprinted. A small windowless room in the back of the Ridgefield police station. As the detectives read him his rights, he sat dazed, trying to keep his composure. "It doesn't get lower than that," he would later tell me, sitting in a holding cell, awaiting a mug shot. He slid toward the center of the bench for the picture and then back out of focus. Hiding.

He watched the detective place each finger, then full palm, onto the top of the fingerprinting machine, then into ink for traditional prints. "Okay, we're done. Go wash your hands," one replied. He wondered why they let him walk down the hallway alone to the restroom until he realized the hallway was locked from the inside out. He was nothing but trapped, with no escape in sight.

75

This is it, I had thought, as I stood in half a foot of snow watching them play. We had driven to Colorado Springs the day prior only to be met with even more snow. Their plastic sleds bounced behind them as they climbed the hill to the side of the resort. The snow was too powdery to gather much speed, so they traveled only a few feet at a time. Smiles and rosy cheeks showed beneath their stocking hats as they pulled themselves out of the snow long enough to look at me with giggles and squeals. I watched Kaylyn mold a snowball with her gloved hand, pitching it toward Riley, who ducked just in time.

This is worth the fight, I thought.

I looked around me. The snow was pure, and I was not. I felt dirty and ragged, chased by shadows of guilt. If I had seen my reflection in the ice hanging from the pines, I would have felt ashamed of the face meeting my gaze. Embittered and disillusioned, angry and spiteful. *Survival instinct is not beautiful,* I had thought, *but it is necessary.* I was drowning in frigid waters with no move left except to hang on, and I didn't like the person I was becoming.

I did not know what tomorrow would bring, but they had today. We were nomads in a foreign winter wonderland with nothing but our suitcases and each other. As I listened to their laughter reverberate across the valley, I wondered if that might actually be just enough to survive.

*****

The gray suit Kyle had borrowed from a friend hung baggily on his skeleton-thin body, as he walked through the avenue of reporters and cameras on November 12. His head hung low to avoid the cameras that were sure to capture his blank stare. The state had placed the case in a domestic violence venue to ensure he had to appear the next day, also allowing more room to maneuver, more space for a hybrid assault manned by both the state's attorney and DCF. I had taken the girls out of the jurisdiction overnight, and this hearing was set up for the state to take control back, with Kyle being the bait. The battle was no longer solely about his actions on July 7. It was about far more.

Reporters sat in the back of the courtroom, state's attorney behind the desk on the right, as Kyle took his place beside Bob on the left. One lone court camera to the side of the judge focused in on him. DCF representatives sat staunchly behind the state's attorney, in show of support. The state's attorney began by explaining DCF's involvement with our family. They had expected us to move in late November, but I had left the state with the children without notifying their representative, and Kyle had consented. That was the hook. The girls were typically under his control, and he had the power to bring them back.

"I am asking that the defendant's conditions of release be modified so he not leave the state of Connecticut; to require that the defendant cooperate with the Department of Children and Families in working with them to return the two children to the state of Connecticut and to provide an immediate address of the children." If Kyle failed in returning the girls to Connecticut, he would do so in violation of a court order. The state's attorney went on to request protective orders against Kyle, which would serve as a court order keeping him away from his family, and the appointment of a guardian *ad litem* for the criminal proceeding, which would displace our authority to make decisions for the girls and allow a third party to engage in further investigations into their lives.

"The state was suggesting they did not know they were moving," Bob inserted, "but there were other circumstances." He gestured toward the back of the courtroom, asking the court to look around the room and outside the courthouse, which was overrun by the media. We were really battling over reasonableness. Would a reasonable person act in a certain way to protect his or her children? He asked the court to consider whether it was a responsible act to extricate the children from this situation. "And to reiterate, the state is asking you to do something that isn't, in all deference to the state, this court's business," he continued. "This is a criminal proceeding." What the state was asking of the court, to involve itself in domestic matters, was outside its venue. DCF was using the power of the state to do that which it could not do on its own, limit individual liberty.

"They are asking you to take away my client's right as a parent to protect her children and raise her children and also speak for her children," Peter inserted. "She strongly opposes that, Your Honor."

*****

I had been staring longingly at the dream-like layers of snow glistening atop the golf course across from our room, the girls watching television in the background, when my phone rang. My entire self-identity hung in the balance before my eyes. I paused before answering, as if to hold on to one more moment of the unknown. As I heard the rushed tone of his voice explaining the outcome of the hearing, I felt my body give way under the relief of a weight removed. I sank deeper into the couch, allowing the flood of tears to finally overcome me. We were safe for the moment. I could breathe. DCF would have to present enough evidence to convince a judge to issue a court order for me to return to Connecticut with the girls. There would be a neutral party. There would be an educated debate on constitutional rights. It was a risk I was willing to take, if it came to that.

"Oh my god, oh my god," the words hung in the cold November air as I ran to hug the girls. My body pulsed with energy. We had won one battle. We were almost there.

*****

We moved into our house later that afternoon. All of our clothes, food, blow-up mattresses, and a bean bag rocker. Friends had begun a charity drive to raise money to find someone to drive the moving truck to Colorado, which still sat motionless in the driveway of our Connecticut home. At night we lay beneath the Colorado stars in our second-story bedroom, blinds raised, mattresses pushed up near the windows. We were not beneath the stars. We were part of the stars, and we were together. As I pulled the blankets up to our chins that first night, I felt pairs of legs on each side lift themselves across mine. We were entangled. We were as one, tumbling through space, among the stars, silent in awe.

76

Evidence of our desperation run through Target lay in plastic bags in the trunk of the car. School supplies. Clothes. Light bulbs. Cleaning supplies. As I pulled my phone out of my pocket to take a seat, I noticed a missed call from a Colorado Springs number. My mind instantaneously ran through the possibilities of who it could be. I leaned up against the hood of the car, anxiously listening to the voicemail from the Colorado Springs police. My body itched with anxiety, my face turned red from anger. I had to stay calm, but I began redialing the number immediately. I was directed to the officer who fielded the call from DCF. He sounded young, with a southwestern accent. The police had been informed that I had fled the state with my children with a criminal trial ongoing. When they stopped by the house, it had appeared empty, he explained. He'd asked a neighbor if anyone lived in our house. I was seething and felt our chances of a normal life, unknown and at peace, slowly slipping away. We were soon to be the new neighbors for whom the police were searching.

"Yes," I said, trying to remain calm, "we haven't been home all day. I even told Rebecca we wouldn't be home. I am out shopping for my children to start school Monday, and yes, our house would look empty. Our furniture is stuck in Connecticut," I said out of frustration, though none of this was his fault.

"So is there a warrant against you or something?"

"No." My voice was escalating, which I self-corrected in an attempt to sound professional and congenial. "There was an accident this summer and my son passed away. My husband was charged this week, and I brought my kids out to Colorado to escape the media frenzy in Connecticut."

"So are you involved in the charges too?" he asked again, confusion growing.

"No! We are part of a superior court proceeding for juvenile matters, but there are no court orders or warrants related to me. It is only my husband. Sir, I'm an attorney and I know how this works. There are other issues at play in Connecticut, and I'm sorry they brought you into it."

"Ma'am, I am too." Consternation and slight annoyance were in his voice. "Honestly, we are short on resources and we have more important things that need my attention than this today. As far as I'm concerned, you are a free citizen and can go wherever you want to go, and I wish you the best. You won't be hearing anything else from us."

I thanked him and returned to the car with an air of relief and slight vindication, which only made me feel guilty. I was being pushed past my limits and found myself calling Rebecca only to be forwarded to voicemail. I had no idea what I would say, but in the blur of emotion my message would relay the effects on the girls of an unexpected police visit at our new home in Colorado. "Do you think *that* is in the best interests of the girls? This has gotten way out of control, Rebecca. It's not even rational anymore." And, as I hung up the phone, I was not rational either. I could have just angered DCF more. I had lost my control, which I had fought so hard to keep. I had long passed the limit of my mind's ability to cope and had finally turned into a rabid animal, bent on survival. I closed the door behind me in shame.

77

They had sat atop their book bags for a picture earlier in the morning of November 17, children bustling into the school on each side of them, bundled in snow gear from the recent storm. My daughters had been uprooted from their home and friends overnight, but I saw no apprehension in their faces, only tentative excitement.

As they walked into the school, I felt as if they were entering the great unknown. A sudden sense of uncertainty, of whether I had made the right decision hit me like lightning. My heart was beating outside my body. I had not let them out of my sight for over a week. I had to let them go, though, and I knew they would be safe. I had talked to the principal and therapist as soon as I arrived in town.

Smiles later greeted me at pick-up, and a frenzy of commentary filled the air on the drive home. As I turned the corner onto our street, the short-lived thrill fell to the wayside as I felt my stomach drop with a rush of adrenaline. A small car was parked along the road outside our house. The only people who would be paying unexpected visits to our house were the police, who we knew were no longer an issue, and Colorado Child Protective Services. A young woman stepped out of the car, early twenties, long brown hair and a smile. I pulled into the garage and cut her off at the top of the driveway, ushering the girls quickly into the house to play with my parents, who were visiting to help us settle in.

"Mrs. Seitz?"

"Yes."

"Hi, I'm Danielle Stephenson from Child Protective Services. I just want to talk with you and your girls a little bit. We received a referral from Connecticut DCF."

"I'm sure you did. Listen, we need to talk up front about this whole situation before you meet with the girls. Okay?" I guided her inside as we stood in the kitchen to discuss the ongoing petition. "I'm sorry we don't have other furniture. It's not a problem. We do have furniture. It's just that… Kyle can't leave the state, so our belongings are still in our driveway."

"That's fine." She smiled. *She seems excited about her job,* I thought, as if she wanted to make a difference in people's lives. I felt a sense of hope when she spoke.

"Listen, I'm just going to speak honestly. I'm happy to give you whatever releases and information you need. I'll even get you the entire file from Connecticut. I *want* you to read through it in detail. I guess you know what happened to our son?"

"Yes, I know enough about the situation to have a discussion."

I explained the facts of the day to her, emphasizing the details of my husband's actions.

"He had been a stay-at-home dad. The kids are his life," I told her. "So we were moving to Colorado in late November anyway. I can send you the signed lease as proof. When he was charged, I just went ahead and left with the girls a week early, to protect them from the media frenzy and hurtful comments at school."

"I can understand that. So are you involved in charges too?"

"No, I didn't do anything that day. I've been keeping the family together. These are my children. We are a loving family. Listen, a lot of political issues are going on in Connecticut. There has been a lot of pressure on both sides for certain things to happen. I just want you to be neutral. That's all I ask." I paused, hearing the girls' laughter upstairs. "To be honest, here's the thing. I haven't let DCF touch the girls because of that. The laughter. I don't want them to know this form of negativity in life. To be involved with child protective services, being interviewed, asked horrible questions. When you talk to them, please just remember that." I led her upstairs to the master bedroom, where the girls were playing on the blow-up mattress. As I closed the door behind me to walk outside and wait for her to return, my heart paused mid-air with a mix of desperation and hope. *Please, please,* I thought.

After a few minutes, she walked out into the garage with a smile on her face.

"How did it go?" I asked anxiously.

"Lindsey, they are the sweetest girls. I had to stop my interview. I couldn't continue asking them the questions I was supposed to. They are just such happy kids."

A rush of emotion crawled up my chest to my face. "Oh, thank you. You have no idea."

"Yeah, I asked them how they were disciplined. They both said you take away toys or electronics, and then your oldest turned to her sister and said, 'No! She takes sugar away from you!' and they both rolled on the mattress laughing."

"So where do we go from here?"

"Let me talk to my supervisor and review your file. I'll need to speak to Kyle if he comes out here, and I need to talk to their principal."

"Okay, and I'll send you all my records of psychiatrist and therapist letters, anything you need."

"That's perfect. I'm sorry this is happening to you; they seem like such wonderful girls. This case has to be open for thirty days, and we need to do our own due diligence. We won't be bothering you with visits, so try to relax and enjoy your new home."

The weight of dread began to slowly extricate its grasp on my body. As an afterthought, I asked her if I could see the report that was made to her. Something inside of me needed to know what was being said behind closed doors.

"I'm not supposed to show you this. You normally have to request a copy, but take a quick look. You can't copy it down though."

I took the paper out of her hands as she turned her back to me, giving me privacy to read.

78

Lindsey has a history of bipolar, and she has been in treatment since she was a teenager. She has a history of making poor choices as a result of her bipolar. She is supposed to be medicated, but [reporting party] isn't sure if she is taking medication.

I was a trapped animal, thrashing to be freed and tormented throughout. I cried, trying to discern how a state agency could relay such an inaccurate and unsubstantiated description of my life. Bloodied and beaten, and all of my own making. I did not need a brain to feel this. It was primal, bred into the very bones of my body. I wanted to be and not be me, to live, but not like this. To crawl into another's skin and hide. Or to crawl inside myself and disappear. I had no way out.

I had become a physical rendering of a scream. Frothy and turbulent. I visualized a lifetime of standing on the edge of the rocky cliffs that now existed above our house, leaning, hands splayed toward the sky. A primal scream.

What do you want from me? What do you want me to say? The words would have reverberated through the canyon, edged with blood and pain. I could not exorcise my demons. They had become me.

Do you want me to say it? I would have screamed toward the sky. *I'm not like you. I'm imperfect, but I'm human. I'm a good mother. A good attorney, wife, mother. Here. Here I am. Come take me, destroy me if it means that much to you.*

*****

Within months of Ben's birth the postpartum illness began, hastened by sleepless nights, breast feeding, and oscillating hormones. When he was four months old, I found myself pacing through our foyer, agitated and depressed, as the visions flashed through my head like lightning. As quickly as they came, they merged with another thought and were gone, as I ran into the kitchen. I was in the depths of postpartum depression.

"Help. You've got to help," I said to Kyle, my voice escalating, agitation evident. I squirmed as if insects were invading my body. All of my muscles were engaged, and I was slowly losing my mind.

"Okay, okay, calm down," he responded, trying to touch me as I jerked away.

Riley then rushed into the kitchen with overly dramatic tears. A missing toy, a television show she didn't want to watch.

"I can't take this," I told him. "Make it stop."

As Kyle ushered her out of the room, calmly talking to her, another vision appeared. I grabbed my phone to call my therapist. "I'm going to take myself to the hospital if you can't fix this! What's happening to me?" I asked her as I paced outside near the car. I would find another psychiatrist soon. I would stop fighting the fact that I had a mental illness. I was experiencing the worst a postpartum illness could bring. I had to get better; my son lay asleep in his crib upstairs. I had to be a mother for him. Kyle could not do it alone. I could not keep pretending around others that I was fine. I could not keep hiding.

*****

It had not been my first bout of postpartum illness. Riley's birth had brought with it a wholly new experience, tinged with paranoia and depression. We had bonded immediately after birth. With fluid matting down her curly hair, she had looked up at me with big brown, soulful eyes, as if to say, "Hey, Mommy!" Yet as I rocked her one afternoon in our townhome in Morrisville, North Carolina, I felt as if I did not even know her. The postpartum depression had forced us to drift apart. I was a third-year law student, studying and walking with her all night. I slept fitfully and had begun to fall apart. The paranoia presented as extreme and irrational worries that were grounded in reality. I feared I was being poisoned by benign household items, like dish detergent, which would in turn poison my daughter through breast feeding. It was an overexaggerated response to normal fears. I was nonfunctional.

I had begun Wellbutrin to see if it helped without having to return to the mood stabilizers I dreaded. I was a few weeks into my regime as I rocked her that afternoon. I began to sing to her. "You are my sunshine…" I noticed her jump and stop sucking from the bottle as her eyes widened looking up at my face. *Had I done something wrong?* I wondered, worried, until a grin spread across her face. I realized I had never sung to her. I was her mother, depressed and sick, and had never sung to my child. I looked off into the distance with a blank stare as I continued singing. I had not taught her the beauty in life, that the world is sound. I had not even been her mother.

79

June 2013

Shelly and I sat together on a wooden bench near the fire pit at the lake watching the sunset. The kids played in the distance, and our friends milled about talking and laughing. Kyle was rocking Ben to sleep in the quiet, beneath a river birch. They were dancing together, father and son. Each time Ben spat his pacifier out, I saw Kyle bend over and pick it up out of the sand, grab another one from the diaper bag, and continue walking and singing. As the sun turned fire orange, tears began to form.

"What's wrong?" she asked, putting her arm around me.

"I don't know. I just feel like I have so much potential, but I can't reach it because of my limitations, and it hurts. I guess I just wish my life was different." I had quit my job in New York City and taken an in-house position at a pharmaceutical company in town, meaning more sleep and more time with my family. I now had more of a work-life balance, but the postpartum depression was overtaking my life during my leave time. I was determined to get better before returning to work.

I had found myself at a deficit in a large law firm compared to other attorneys. We were judged based upon billable hours, and I often found myself working weekends on end, sleeping on the bare floor in my office, commuting three hours a day, taking trains home at 1 a.m. to sleep three hours just to finish the work in the morning. Other attorneys could handle the hours, but I found the lack of sleep and relaxation were precursors to bouts of depression. My moods ranged. Sometimes I experienced what seemed to be hypomania or at least periods of stability where I found deep happiness in my job, taking on many projects, proving that I could work with the best of the best. As a female with children, I felt as if I bore the burden of proving it could be done, and I largely succeeded. However, the good times would always be followed by darkness, where I mourned the time I did not get to spend with my children who were growing up before my eyes, questioning the path of my life, yearning for something more meaningful. No matter the time, though, I always felt like I was running uphill, trying to keep up with certain limitations that made the playing ground quite uneven.

My illness never interfered with my job and I garnered an extreme professionalism, yet it had more subtle repercussions. I often said Kaylyn saved my life, as her birth in 2006 ushered me into adulthood, forcing me to gain control over my illness to engage in a meaningful career and motherhood. The intense moods and irresponsibleness of my adolescence ended, and I largely coped in remission with milder symptoms for years. Yet as I sat with Shelly that summer evening, I had no idea how to move forward in life, as the struggles over the past three years, in particular the postpartum times, had become unmanageable.

"I know. I can only imagine," she said quietly, "but you know, you have so many gifts. You are a beautiful person."

I allowed myself to cry in her arms as we watched the sun set over the lake.

80

Follow up with police regarding if mother is being charged.

It was the last recommendation made to our new caseworker when the file was transferred with the submission of the neglect petition in court. I overlooked the sentence the first time I read the file, with it eliciting only a passing irritation, but over the months as my mind calmed, I began to focus on what those words really meant. It was the end of August by the time that recommendation was made, and DCF's investigation had been completed. They knew the truth of July 7. I was not involved in any care of Ben that day. The morning routine, drop off, pickup, was in Kyle's wheelhouse. I would often wonder what they thought I could have been charged with. Not having contemplated the unimaginable that day in order to stop the passage of time? Was the accident so unbelievable that I had to be involved in some way? Or was it the simple fact of my having a mental illness?

I could not wholly blame DCF, though. It was only a symptom of a broader ailment. The utterance of the word "mental illness" in hushed tones behind closed doors. Like a leper, not to be touched. Something if avoided, to disappear into the night. I had seen discussions of mental illness appear more often recently, due to the increasing frequency of mass violence. School shootings. Debates as to which to blame—guns or mental illness. We had failed society though, in cloaking mental illness with a shroud of secrecy, only brought to light in rare cases of violence, allowing the majority of Americans with mental illnesses to suffer in silence under the weight of stigmatization. It was something to be feared, abnormal, pushed under the rug.

I read those words in the report while I was struggling with my own journey of self-acceptance. I stared at the paper before me, confused. Who was I? I was a mother, wife, friend, neighbor, colleague. I was neither dangerous nor negligent with others' lives, but on the day my son died, I was more than that to many people. A nurse in the emergency room the night of Ben's death had immediately reported my illness. That night, I was more than a grieving mother. I was mentally ill.

81

Kyle lay alone in our now-barren Connecticut home. A chair in the corner, a few dishes for lunches, a twin-size blow-up mattress and some clothes. Our new therapy dog, a golden retriever named Harley, napped in his pen beside him, constantly scratching to be let out to do his job—to give therapy and love. Many nights, he lay on the mattress with Harley curled up beside him, staring out the window into the cold, windy New England night, the branches of the large oak trees in our yard being tossed to and fro. There was no longer the smell of life in the house, only the musty smell of age and wood. Of a life that was.

He had lost even more weight and withdrawn into a shell of himself, avoiding friends, avoiding the world. Friends were worried, and I was too. I could not fathom the depths of his depression. He had stopped seeing his therapist, and I wondered if he was just waiting to die with no hope left. But I knew he was strong. Stronger than me. He had never questioned life like I had, other than fleeting intellectual contemplations of suicide. He had held firm, trusted our love, and continued on. Yet I could not help a racing heart, in those groggy moments between dreaming and wakefulness at night, when I heard my phone vibrate. Is this the phone call where a friend whispers, "Lindsey, it's Kyle."

*****

A few days after his plea of not guilty, I sat alone in our living room in Colorado, also listening to the gusts of snowy wind blowing the pines against our house. I felt barren and cold in a season of love. We had been warned that the state's attorney would fight against his being able to visit us during the holidays. With him in Colorado, they lost all leverage of getting the girls back or negotiating a quick plea bargain. I would not allow the girls' feet to hit Connecticut soil until the investigations were over for fear of losing them, so we had resigned ourselves to holidays spent alone.

My parents had offered to stay with us until Kyle returned, and they spent all their time trying to make the holidays bearable for the girls and me, but they were attempting to do the impossible. We had seen some glimpses of hope in positive interactions with Colorado CPS, but our attorneys had also received a threat from Connecticut DCF to try and have us ordered to return back to Connecticut. The despondency I felt sitting by the window that night, though, was less about the investigations than it was the loss of our only strength—our family unit.

We had been offered time to grieve for our son only in short bursts of peace. We had devoured those moments, as if famished, and I found myself still hungry and unsatisfied. We had seen the holidays approaching before Kyle was charged and had prepared ourselves for surviving the first season without Ben's giggles as he tore apart wrapping paper and we placed red bows on his head.

The holidays were mystical for our family, and this year in particular we needed to be carried away to another world of love and hope. Thanksgiving with the smell of fresh roasting turkey and sweet potato soufflé, the sound of the Macy's Thanksgiving Day parade in the background, the touch of hands interlocked in prayer. Black Friday with Kyle struggling to ensure our fresh-cut Christmas tree made it onto the baler with all branches intact, the girls' eyes glittering with excitement. Christmas music and rosy cheeks on the ride home, a rush of energy and joy as the girls placed ornaments in just the right places on the tree. The vision had been close enough to touch, a resting place in the future where we could heal.

I did not know how to tell the girls that their father would not be home for the holidays, that the path we had carefully forged for holiday healing would not occur this year. That our rebuilding would have to wait. As I watched the snowflakes fall outside our window, the promise of what was to be existed no more. I could not mutter the truth that the doorbell would not ring, no matter how much they prayed for their father to come home. I began to wonder if maybe the holidays weren't limited to a time and place; possibly the holidays truly were a state of mind. Maybe it is the simple love of God, a light in the darkness that existed around us every day of the year. Still, I did not feel consoled.

82

"You become. It takes a long time. That's why it doesn't happen often to people who break easily, or have sharp edges, or who have to be carefully kept."[22] It was a quote from *The Velveteen Rabbit* I'd seen on a picture frame I had just purchased that got me thinking, and as we drove home, I knew only that I had not become. I was so far from becoming that I had lost all hope of it ever occurring. I was mired in grief and desperation.

I had been walking through a local Christmas shop with my mother when the walls closed in on me. Christmas music blared from the speakers, and with a blaze of memories, I was swept back in time. I could feel Ben again, as if he was walking beside me but just out of reach. In a parallel universe, I felt the day as it could have been: our family walking around the shop together, the girls brimming with joy picking out ornaments, Ben toddling around touching anything that was shiny. I would lift him up, my arms encircling his chubby stomach, and kiss his cheeks. "No, Benja," I would say laughingly and place him on my hip, our faces nearly touching. I would feel his sweet breath, smell his hair.

"I can't do this. I don't know *how* to do this." I had turned to my mother, tears streaming down my cheeks. To escape the Christmas memories, I marched upstairs to the discount room, feigning interest just to allow my mother enough time to continue looking downstairs. My eyes settled on a blue picture frame with writing scrawled along the edges. "It doesn't happen all at once," it said. "Generally, by the time you are Real, most of your hair has been loved off, and your eyes drop out and you get loose in the joints and very shabby. But these things don't matter at all, because once you are Real you can't be ugly, except to people who don't understand." I so desperately wanted that, to be real, so I grabbed the frame instinctively, paid for it, and made a hasty exit.

As we drove home, though, the words had cut something deep. Opened up an old wound.

"I still feel like this can't be real. You know?" I told my mother, crying. "The aftermath has been a trauma in itself. I could never have imagined this. I just need to grieve." I had uncovered a torrent of emotion.

"We feel like prisoners of war," I told her. We were gulping any breath of fresh air offered to us, before the water flowed over our faces again. Every day, I lived on eggshells, woke up anxious. Our adrenal glands were nearing exhaustion, a rush of cortisol with each phone call or email. "I can't take much more." I pulled off to the side of the road unable to drive.

Ben had "become." Actually, he simply *Is*, and always was, real in full living color and vibrancy. I had not, however, become anything but a trapped animal, going through the motions of life. I felt fragmented, not whole, and yearned so deeply to just be me. To become real. Yet I was so very far away.

*****

Two days later, I crested the hill in Bear Creek (a nature park near our house) on a jog, gasping for breath. I bent over with my hands on my knees, feeling the sharp wind against my skin. My face was burning from the cold. I needed to breathe, and I simply could not. I was alone, miles from home with no way to return except the way I had come. I continued down the path in anguish.

"I can't take much more. I'm saying it out loud. I'm at my true breaking point; as a human, I can't last much longer." I spoke the words to Ben, my grandparents, Kyle's mother, God, anyone who would listen.

If there was a Heaven, if they were listening, I was finally talking. There was nothing left but to talk. No one but me, alone and in the universe. I visualized the cliffs above our house, the precipitous fall. I needed something to give, or I would. I was truly at my breaking point. Yet as I picked up my pace, I felt a certain relief in the talking, to someone, or something, far away from me in this physical world.

83

As I looked at the picture frame of Ben sitting on the mantle above our fireplace, I often wondered what it meant to become and how it was accomplished. I had been unbecoming for so long, I could not imagine what it would feel like to be me, or even find me. Who was "me" anyway, this "self" that people referred to in passing? The notion of the self as something that transcends the body is age old—from the burial rights of Neanderthals and ancient Egyptian concepts of multiple souls to the immortal soul central to Vedic Brahmanism. However, theories of what the self or soul is and its role in our life vary greatly.

Hinduism teaches that the self or soul (Atman) is consciousness, the very center of who we are, surviving reincarnations until it reunites with universal consciousness (Brahman) from which it came. Karmic reincarnations serve as the self's journey to recognize this oneness with Brahman. Buddhism, on the other hand, teaches that there is no afterlife because there is no self or soul to begin with. Reality and the self are all illusions. In the Tibetan tradition however, there is a part of us called *rigpa* or "core consciousness," and the entire goal of our many lives is to recover knowledge of this core essence, when it can then break free of cyclical existence and vanish into the clear light of pure awareness.

The rise of Abrahamic theology brought with it a different view. The individual soul is central to Christianity. A soul that falls into the physical world, struggles through life to merge once again into a condition of divinity. It is a personal, individual journey. It is our heart of hearts, and through it we are connected to God. The Kingdom of God is within us.

I thought back to what I had witnessed in the funeral home. There was a soul which had left Ben's body, and it was personal. The body I witnessed was not Ben. He was absent. I was reminded of the internal dissonance I experienced on a daily basis. I was not yearning each moment of my life to be a state of emptiness. I was yearning to be something. To be "me." In both cases, the absence of a self taught me it existed. I felt desperately estranged from my own self, as if she walked beside me each day, and I had to find a way to make that connection, no matter the cost. I was just not sure how.

Romantics view our alienation as something to be conquered through development of our own individuality. Finding and allowing "me" to evolve, by becoming the complete spiritual being I was always supposed to be. In some circles, evolution is not conceived in purely physical terms anymore. Evolution now encompasses spirituality as well. "The Universe" says Ernest Holmes, "is a Spiritual System ... the entire Cosmos is (or may be) reflected in [man's] mind! Evolution is the awakening of the soul to a recognition of its unity with the Whole."[23] Material evolution is only an effect. The spirit (wholeness, God, cosmic consciousness), the soul (personal medium of divinity), and the body (physical vessel of evolution). The Christian Trinity also embodies the concept of God as one—the Father, Son, and Holy Ghost. Therefore, in a world of the personal soul, which is evolving, humans can find meaning in the day-to-day. Evolving and becoming our true selves in the eyes of God is the entire reason for the journey.

I still did not have the slightest idea how to evolve spiritually in a physical world, though. I knew I felt positive energy and negative energy at various times in my life. Harmony and resonance within when I acted out of love, spent time with my family and friends, and engaged in acts that were central to who I was as a person. Dissonance within when I acted out of anger or revenge, with lies, if I hurt someone, when family time was lacking, and, most importantly, when I denied my true self.

I largely overlooked my intuitive gauge, passing it off as just feelings, nothing more, and relying on what I thought mattered, my brain and rationality. But what if I had been wrong all along? If God was in my heart, why should I not rely on my gut feelings along with my rational brain? If my soul was evolving, the only place to look was inward, and I needed to use those feelings to guide my actions as well. I needed to get my hands dirty in the nitty-gritty of life each and every day, to work and evolve.

84

Colorado was supposed to bring me closer to Ben, but I only felt myself drifting further and further away. I was becoming tired and numb from the battles waging back in Connecticut, and it was hard to concentrate on anything else. So when I received the news the Monday after Thanksgiving that DCF was dropping our petition and leaving it up to Colorado CPS whether or not to open a new case, the relief passed in an instant and I only sank deeper into a daze.

Through contentious back and forth negotiations and in the absence of a DCF petition, the state's attorney had agreed to allow Kyle to quietly join us in Colorado. Yet when he walked into our house on December 6, I felt nothing but a sense of estrangement from him and the world. I no longer knew him, at least no more than I knew myself. I had grown so disillusioned from the constant fighting that I had lost all sense of reality and meaning. I visualized the world orbiting the sun with tiny black forms scurrying to and fro, mindlessly, frantically chasing something or someone.

My mind kept coming back to the quote by philosopher William James: "We are like islands in the sea, separate on the surface but connected in the deep." We were living in an age of isolation. A reality forged by human hands, yet in conflict with the truth that lies beneath. The dissonance had become deafening. I felt as if I had seen so much discord in such a short amount of time. I could not help but question where we had all gone wrong. Aristotelian thinkers in a quantum world. Polarization when we would be better served by compromise and creativity. I had seen so much useless pain instead of empathy and compassion.

I could pinpoint myself on the map, a tiny black form, sitting, tired from the battle, wishing rather to just surrender with a sigh of exhaustion. I was quickly becoming disillusioned with life itself. Something had to change, and the only place to start was with me.

85

I was learning how to rebuild our lives, but I did not yet know how to rebuild love. Riley sat atop Kyle's shoulders, pink-striped running shirt and a grin, threads of hair falling into her face, as he bounced her along the trail in front of me. Kaylyn led our hike, being dragged by Harley, who sprinted ahead, happy to finally be at home and in the wild.

I could not decide what love attaches to and whether it was still there. Not the physical, for I could not yet stand for him to touch me. He stood on the other side of the river bed, waiting for me to cross, offering his hand, which I denied. I'd rather it stay that way, a deep chasm between us, which he had dug himself. Not emotions, for only apathy filled the space where affection had once lived. As he continued walking, I slowed to allow the distance to build between us again.

He deposited Riley onto the dirt, as all four of them ground to a halt. I arranged them, kneeling together, for a picture. No, there must be a deeper attachment, for as I snapped the photograph, I felt no familiar emotion at all on the surface, and certainly not love. Love had to be somewhere else, somewhere deeper, in a place I had yet to venture.

I had thought of what divorce would mean for us in passing one night, and I could not decipher its meaning. My children losing that which made them whole, being shuttled between the two of us. I would live apart from someone I still cared for deeply, but do it just out of spite, to prove something. That he did not deserve forgiveness. Friday movie nights, lunch dates, laughter, my shoulder to cry on. All gone.

A core of love remained hidden deep within us, linking us together, and I had to work to figure out how to nourish it again.

*****

I owed it to the girls to discover whether I could love the same person but differently. If a new kind of love could grow from the kernel left behind in the rubble. We took small steps as a family at first, which included our first night out at a local resort, resting at the base of Cheyenne Mountain. It housed a restaurant with a bowling alley and gaming stations, and the entire resort was already decorated for Christmas with white lights outlining the evergreens along the lake, trees and wreaths decorated throughout. I had hoped decorations and activities would redirect their attention from my apprehension.

I sat at the high-top table sipping a Christmas cosmopolitan with gas logs roaring behind me. I watched the girls run between appetizers and bowling, giggling along the way. Kyle helped Riley drag the bowling ramp onto the alleyway since she lacked the strength to roll a bowling ball independently. The apprehension slowly melted as I began to notice pieces of us floating around in the action. I felt an emptiness in the air, but it wasn't swallowing us whole as I had expected. Becoming engrossed in the girls' frivolity was forcing Kyle to loosen up as well; I heard more laughter and joking as the night progressed, and as we exited the resort, I caught Riley tackling him in the lobby of the hotel, wrestling him to the ground, where she jumped on his back for a ride. It was living, and that was good enough for the moment.

*****

We only had a few days until he would have to fly back to Connecticut for his next appearance, so we spent the time we did have together preparing for Christmas. My mind retraced our steps back a year, back to the rural Christmas tree farm where we hiked to cut our Frasier fir. Ben rode in the Baby Björn, just the height where his head rested right below my nose, as I lowered my face ever so often to feel the soft threads of hair on my skin, attempting to catch a sniff of his baby smell. It was comforting. We were merry, sipping hot cider while picking out garland and wreaths. Life was good.

This Christmas, though, we found ourselves walking through the outdoor gardening center of Home Depot, Kyle standing each tree up at its full height and us giving it a thumbs up or thumbs down. We wanted a large tree, to fit as much festivity as we could into our holiday, and we were pleased as we drove home.

As Kyle set up the tree in front of our arch window and I sat with the girls unpacking ornaments, Christmas music rang out from our speaker system. I gradually sank into a deep pool of reminiscence until my mind fell away and nothing was left except the moment at hand. My two remaining children, scurrying about in their pajamas, gently lifting ornaments in amazement, "Mom! Look at this one!" We may not have been complete that night, but we were still a family.

86

I examined my husband's face as the four of us sat on the couches waiting for the girls' new psychologist to lead us through our first family therapy session. He seemed unsure but ready to try anything. He was settling in, happy to be home. A quote sent from a friend two months after Ben's death ran through my head as I watched him hug Kaylyn around her waist and pull her closer. "It might be more accurate to call them a marriage of true minds. They're just the most wonderful and joyous couple… You feel good when you're around them."[24] Our friends who knew us before Ben's death yearned for us to return to the way we were. They wanted us to feel *that* love again, the love that gave our hearts strength to fight to the ends of the earth for the sake of it. I wanted that love back too, but I wasn't sure it still lived in this new world. Tiny intricacies of our love had become unwoven, and I was desperately trying to pull the threads back together. I was willing to try, though, and knew it would entail one small step at a time.

The therapist walked into the room and introduced herself, shaking our hands and joking with the girls. She then turned to pull a card game off the shelf beside her desk, *Truth or Dare*. "Let's start with a game," she announced.

I was not an actor, and she could sense consternation in my tentative response. Kaylyn, however, was first to jump off the couch and draw a card. She raced to the opposite side of the room, making space for her stage, placed her headband on backward, which lifted the back of her hair up to flow down over her forehead. She then strutted across the room, shaking her bum back and forth, hand on hip, saying in her best model accent, "Oh, yeah. I'm awesome." She turned to blow a kiss to her admirers, which prodded Riley to join in.

"Runway model!" we all screamed, as the room exploded with laughter.

Then it was my turn, as I hesitantly pulled a card out of the deck. "Imitate a golfer," it said. I grabbed my putter, dropped the ball on the ground, stepped back to aim, bent over a bit, shaking my bum just like Kaylyn, saying in my most helpless girl voice, "Oh, I just don't know how to putt... Honey, can you come show me?" We all vibrated with energy. If but for an instant, our minds had forgotten.

Over time, I noticed a slow but sure evolution taking place. We had to put the work in, and it would take time, but we were beginning to weave together a new us, in our new life. A joke here and there, more inappropriate quips flying between us as we drove down the road. More laughter filling the house. The threads may have been splayed, but they were still present.

We spent a quiet Christmas together in our new home. There was pain in the empty space surrounding us, but there was joy too, and on New Year's Eve after dinner at a local resort, my eyes fell upon two little girls, jiving on the dance floor and squealing with delight. Their father was laughing as well, arm extended, twirling them in circles, as they all held hands. A slight grin crossed my face. That is *my* family, I thought with pride as the clock ticked off the seconds of a year I could not get back.

87

A warm Spring day in New England, dogwoods in bloom, the smell of fresh grass beneath our feet. Ben toddling out onto the soccer field, blue and gray striped shirt, stomach showing. The game played on. I ran after him, grabbing him across his chest and flying him back to the sidelines, belly laughs. When his feet hit the ground, turning and running back toward the field, arms held out for balance, I chased. After the game, we sat with family friends on a restaurant patio for a late lunch. The breeze blowing our napkins, which we weighted down. Laughter and horseplay between the children. They followed Ben around the patio as the adults finished eating. Kaylyn sat beside him on the curb of the flower bed as he played with a napkin. When he concentrated on an object in his hands, his cheeks blew out like a puffer fish. He toddled over to his high chair, locking himself in jail with the straps beneath. We all laughed.

I had begun mourning more than Ben. I was mourning the loss of our life. I often found myself processing through old memories of our life in New England. Without blood family around, we made friends our family. Our lives had finally matured, and we were settled.

In the blink of an eye….

I knew I had to let go, make new friends, move on. Yet the memories were magnetic. So when my doorbell rang a week before Christmas, I was less than motivated to answer. A woman stood on my front porch, trying to rein in her small brown dog, who, smelling Harley, was pulling to run into our house. She was taller than me, short blonde hair, pleasant, with a light-hearted smile. She introduced herself as Amber, a neighbor up the street. We chatted through formalities for a few minutes, after which she invited me to a neighborhood ladies bunco night. I liked her, but I remained hesitant.

As the day grew closer, I found myself retreating into myself. I'd never had many close friends. My illness made sure of that, and those I did make, I had just left overnight. I felt an empty hole growing in my chest, and I was not anxious to fill it. Also, the promise of introductions had scared me. Who was I? I didn't know anymore what to tell myself, let alone other people. How many kids did I have? What did I do for a living? My husband? Why did we move?

I am lost, which is how I arrived here.

I have three children, two living, one somewhere or nowhere; I haven't decided yet.

I don't know who I am anymore. I am a deep, dark void.

I eventually acquiesced, and as Amber and I walked together to the party, I concentrated on the ice cracking beneath my feet. The silence of the night. We chatted as I shivered in the cold night air. My nerves running awry. We were some of the first attendees there, and I stole a spot off to the side where I felt safe, not too far away to look antisocial but not in the midst of things. After more women arrived, Amber introduced me as the new neighbor with two girls, and my body relaxed. As the night progressed, my anxiety began to melt. There were jokes and laughter. I still did not know who I was, or who I would be at the end of our journey, but for one night in mid-January, I could just simply be the new neighbor who was lucky at bunco.

88

"Mommy, do you still think about Ben and miss him?" Riley whispered as I snuggled her one night in late January.

I was caught off guard. My breathing stopped. "Of course I do! Why did you ask that?"

"Because you don't talk about him much anymore."

I pulled her closer to me. "I think about him all the time. I talk about him whenever you guys want to, but I don't want to dwell on it. You girls are important to me too. Ben is always here with us, though." I did not want to be the mother who could not move on. I did not want to be the downer anymore. We were laughing again, I focused on that. Not the pain.

She seemed satisfied with my answer, rolling back over to face the window. I watched the rise and fall of her body as she breathed, combing her hair out of her face with my fingers. If she only knew the words I could not say.

Every atom of my body vibrates with the energy of Ben, every moment of every day.

All that I do is subsumed by Ben.

My entire consciousness is Ben. The Ben that was, and the Ben that is.

When I run on the dirt trails, the rhythm of my steps and breath spell his name.

On my worst days, I stop beneath the mountains, tinged red with the setting sun, and speak to him.

"I love you, Ben."

*****

A friend had told me a few months after Ben's death that life moves on whether we want it to or not, a jab to my grieving heart. I mulled over her statement in my mind, trying to decide what those words meant to us in our healing process.

Life = the universe, objective time, our family's life, others' lives

Moves on = forgets, progresses, evolves, follows its prior trajectory

Like it or not = wanting… to rewind time to July 6, 2014, others to stay in the place where we are, our lives to stop because Ben is dead

Maybe the answer lay in her question that night. That we would forever want to rewind time but could not, that we hoped deeply for others' lives to move forward as they were but with a bit of Ben with them. That ours would not, possibly for a lifetime, but that we did not want anyone to ever have to join us in this place, and I knew my daughters were included in the latter group. *Please, please move on, my baby girl,* I thought as Riley drifted off to sleep.

*****

A few weeks later I found myself sitting on our bed, sheets crumpled beneath me, just watching video after video. I feared forgetting. The sound of his voice, the smirk beneath his pacifier as he sucked feverishly. The deep wrinkles in his legs from his baby fat, the freckle on his left foot.

His stomach protrudes beneath his shirt like a watermelon as he walks along the pathway at the concert in the park the prior June. Plaid shorts, white striped shirt, blue sandals. He palms a yellow football in his left hand. Would he have been left-handed?

"Throw the ball, Ben. Throw it!" I say to him, video-taping his toddle across the grass toward his sister, who is waiting with open arms. He stops, teeter-totters, regains his balance, looks around at the crowd. "Throw it Ben!" He stops again. "Ahhhhh," he screams with glee. Trumpets play in the background, children laughing and playing. He glances up at me, grins, and launches it, left-handed.

Mother and son, there was something special about that bond. One soul tugging at the heart of another. Something I knew I could never forget.

89

There were cracks. Ones that had not been there before and which we would have to build around. Some thin and reparable, others deeper and darker. As I tried to wean off Ativan, some of the physiological cracks began to appear more often. An unexpected touch on my shoulder, a bump in the road, a loud noise. One day in January 2015, I remember waking from a particularly restless sleep. The girls were standing by the couch while I scurried around the kitchen making lunches. They were bickering, which soon escalated to yelling and dramatic, cacophonous whining and tears.

With a rush of adrenaline, the crack fissured off in multiple directions, growing, flowing. I felt as if my nerves were glaringly raw to the world. Kaylyn's blue-green book bag sat on the edge of the kitchen table; I watched as my arm forcefully swept it across the table, tumbling into a chair, which tipped over as Harley scattered amid the clanking of wood against wood.

"Stop, just stop. I can't take this," I yelled as Kaylyn rushed to pet Harley, muttering, "Okay, okay." My body plopped down in the nearest chair, hands on head, as if to cover a gaping wound. I was immediately shocked and disgusted at my outward display of emotion in front of the girls. It had been a tidal wave, and I hadn't seen it coming.

As we pulled into the school parking lot, I unbuckled my seatbelt and spun around to face them, touching their legs to keep them from leaving the car. I told them after Ben died, I was... different. My brain could not handle certain things. It had been the yelling, the loudness of it, like razor-sharp cuts on my nerves. I needed them to understand. It wasn't them, and my behavior wasn't like me. I was sorry.

"Everything that's happened," I paused, searching for the right words. "I am... affected." That was it. The flood gates had opened, the words flowed so effortlessly, as if expunging many demons, of many years past, and not just of death, but more than that.

"Okay." The girls nodded, gave me a kiss, and ran off to class.

Tears flowed freely, cleansing me of a dirty residue of pain and suppression. Why hadn't I been able to say those three words before? I am affected. It had been my coat of armor. Nothing affects me. You cannot hurt me. I had clamped down on any outward show of emotions to the world, even family, in order to survive. To stay strong, to save myself. Any crack, and I would continue to crumble until nothing was left. But it was all a lie. A hardened but breakable shell of me. I could be hurt. I had been hurt, and it did not weaken me. By being real, by being human, I could find strength.

*****

The deeper cracks were convoluted and ragged. "Daddy," he said, a small boy with long brown hair, jumping off the steps of the pool into his father's arms. We were watching the 2015 Super Bowl as the Dove Men+Care® commercial raced across the screen. I had not been prepared, and then there were more boys, growing boys, and fathers. Potty training, "Daddy," clumsily getting undressed, falling off a jungle gym, going to prom, having a baby, "Dad." A toddler crying, it was Ben's cry, and my mind fell out of itself once more. The pain of losing Ben turned inside out as my body convulsed.

Kyle tried to touch me as I squirmed away. "What's wrong with you?" he asked, as I stood at the foot of our couch, blocking the television.

"I despise you sometimes. You know that, right?" I was screaming, gesticulating wildly. "You couldn't even control your thoughts enough to get Ben to daycare!"

"I'm leaving and taking the girls with me. You aren't their father anymore," I continued screaming as I ran into the basement, slamming the door behind me. I continued pacing in the darkness, breathing labored, mind spinning. I should have recognized my breakdown as more than a bout of grief or anger, but I did not, and instead sat in a corner, knees pulled up to my chest, hands in my hair, rocking. "I hate him, I hate him," I screamed through the night air.

90

We visualized it in our minds. How the case would be built. They would have to paint a picture of their making in the jurors' minds of a father and his son. The emergency room physicians would sit uneasily in the witness chair. They would have to start by describing a baby boy, dead upon arrival. Words like *rigor mortis* would be used to shock the jurors, and his temperature, the look of him. Bob would counter with his own picture, of a father screaming, rolled into a primordial ball on the floor in the waiting room. He turned right instead of left, they would say, because of, we don't know what, but it was hectic that morning. Additional people in the house, confusion, noise, rushing around. Isn't that enough? He entered and exited the front seat of his car nine times that day without noticing his son, without ever looking in the back seat. Isn't that evidence of negligence? You don't look in the back of a car at a rear-facing infant seat without reason, though, we would say. He stood in line for a sandwich at lunch, bored, clicking emails on his phone, reading nothing important on the internet while his son lay dead in the car, they would counter. Can you picture it yet?

He drove to daycare and walked into the toddler's room. "Where's Ben?" They would present daycare workers as witnesses. He walked to the next room, thinking, *Ben is in that room, I'm sure of it.* The daycare worker would testify she wondered why the father was there. "Ben's not here today," she had informed him. *What do you mean Ben is not here today,* he thought. *Did Lindsey come get him? Am I confused;*

did she keep him home today? Then they would describe the physical manifestation of his mind falling out of itself too. He had picked up speed as he walked out of the daycare to his car, a witness would relay. She heard a scream. At first, she thought it was a child but then realized it was a man, and she saw the head of a baby, with long, curly blond hair, as the man tried to shake him awake, screaming, "Oh my god, oh my god!" And he would speed away. Away, away into the sun. Wheels squealing on asphalt. Why did he not call 911? That is evidence of negligence too, they would say. But he had already lost his mind, Bob would counter, as he sped to the hospital, hitting a car on the way. He had called his wife on the way (thank God she didn't answer), but what would he have said?

There was a urine smell in the car that he should have recognized; police would debate, one by one, whether there was or not. The primordial ball of a man, screaming. He would tell hospital staff, "You have to find my wife, physically collect her and bring her here. I'm scared she will kill herself." In this manner, a picture would be painted, of a father and son. He had been a stay-at-home father, Bob would say and witnesses would support; his son was his life. He was the epitome of a loving father. Experts would be presented. It is a well-known fault of memory. It has been researched and proven, they would say. However, there would still be a grotesque picture placed as a centerpiece in the courtroom, and our lives in the balance. There would be two little girls, whose lives depended on their father being free, with them.

So we would plea. The visualization, the burden of our story being placed on others, headlines in papers, was too much to bear. Above all else, we were tired. Tired of fighting and unsure of what we were fighting about, or for, anymore. Unsure of whether my mental illness would be made public, if I would be pulled into the sparring too. A new emotion was beginning to take over our lives. It was a deep longing, a tiny thread to lift us out of the darkness. A need to consider *why* we were making decisions and *who* it would affect, *what* it would mean in the end. A desire to take what was given to us and act in the opposite manner. There was nothing left but to look up into the light.

*****

As Kyle strode into the courtroom on March 10, he was setting us free. We had nothing left but the ability to mold our response to the world, and he had taken part of his humanness back. It was a new beginning. We had found power, not in winning, but in recognizing that winning was not the end game. He pleaded under the Alford doctrine, not admitting guilt but recognizing that the prosecution had enough evidence to convict him. The prosecution accepted it with open arms. There was always going to be a plea, Bob had told us; they never wanted to take this to trial. So a guilty finding would be made on the record, and there would be a sentencing. Part of his spirit needed absolution, but of a type that he would not find in a courtroom. It was a form he could only find within himself.

91

With the plea taken and suspended sentence, meaning no probation or jail time, it was finally just about Ben. I felt as if he were inside of me, pulling my body inward, toward him. I was twisted and knotted. We were entangled, and his grasp was firm. As I lay sprawled across his grave, staring at the stars, I felt only the cold, firm earth beneath my body. It was his second birthday, and I had to be with him. My body retched its soul into the night sky as it crawled and groveled to touch him again. There had not been an ample saying of our goodbyes. One last kiss was missing, and the hole in my heart that existed was imploding inward.

I pictured the night he was born. When he decided to come, it happened fast. The trees passed in a blur as we sped through dark, country roads to the nearest hospital. Contractions were already two minutes apart, and the pressure was unbearable. I told Kyle to pull the car over, as I thought we could not make it to the hospital, but he was determined to continue driving until we were parked in front of the maternity ward. Ben was born ten minutes after our arrival. The doctor held him up. "It's a boy!" I was amazed at the sight, so pink, healthy.

"Oh my God, he's so beautiful," I had said in awe. It was an angelic beauty.

"You can't call him that," Kyle said laughing. "He's a dude. He's handsome!"

His scream had been so loud, so alive. But when they placed him in my arms, he carried a calm with him. I looked down at him. "Hey Benjamin, it's Mommy," I whispered, pulling back his stocking hat. He turned his head toward my voice, and in that moment, I fell in love.

Yet as I lay with him that night, two years later, he was gone. He was not in my arms nor beneath me. He was somewhere else. "Hey, Benjamin, it's Mommy," I whispered one last time into the night sky. "I love you."

*****

I had hoped my visit back to Connecticut would bring comfort and healing in a time of spiritual mourning, but it only ushered in more angst. I had landed to ice and snow, both physically and spiritually. I was frigid and on edge. Every piece of earth held a memory, glaring memories of love lost and trauma. *This is where we played in the park for summer concerts,* I thought as I drove down the street. *This is where we ate ice cream as a family. This was the girls' school. I miss, I love, I yearn,* were the emotions running through my mind. I visualized Kyle's car sitting on Main Street that morning as I drove by. Ben was alive, babbling in the back seat. And I kept driving. It was a prison of memories, and I just wanted to return to Colorado as soon as possible.

92

We were our own arbiters of guilt, and we would continue to wrestle with its intricacies for a lifetime. The contours of the day were so variegated and complex that no single conclusion seemed appropriate. It was a day that blended all that is human into one, like paint on a canvas, creating a picture that held within its form another meaning entirely. One that when analyzed from afar appeared drastically different than when viewed up close. In an intimate fashion.

The train often lulled us to sleep as it swayed back and forth on the tracks. The sporadic screech of its horn not breaking through the fog of pure exhaustion. I watched other commuters, wondering who they had left at home and where they were going. Whether it was worth it. The woman with papers lying in her lap, which kept sliding to the ground as she nodded off. Her head bobbing. I had long since resolved within my own mind that it was not worth it for me at this point in my career with two young children, that I needed more time with family, but I had kept riding for all too long. Walking the four blocks from Grand Central, masses of people in suits and high heels, jostling about. Rushing toward something important. The pungent smell of metal and cars floating up from the ground. Only when I found out I was pregnant with Ben did I quit my job in the city and settle in closer to home, but I had been unhappy for some time. Maybe in the future I could pursue my career goals, but at that time with young children, I had met my match.

Since my law school years, I had been torn. Struggling to find the right balance. I was in a better place to support our family while Kyle took on the role as the stay-at-home parent, and I was fulfilled by a career. Yet like many women of my generation, I felt a stronger tug toward my family. My soul was invested in my children, and I could not bear to miss any milestones in their lives. So we patched it together over time. I rushed home for bedtime routines before logging back on for a late night of work, telecommuting from home as much as possible to attend school plays and soccer games, surprise lunches at school. Early dinners and family game nights on Fridays. Every moment of each day was carefully planned and allocated between work and family. Kyle and I rarely made it out on our own, but we were happiest as a close-knit clan of five, inseparable. We felt complete that way.

Over time I had begun to wear down. Too little sleep, too much time being pulled away unexpectedly from the kids for work. Ben died the Monday after the Fourth of July holiday. A day I had just needed to rest. A break from years of exhaustion and long hours at work, a short respite for myself. It was so very simple, what I had hoped for. Ben would be happily playing at daycare, the girls at Vacation Bible School. I would have a few hours with a book and coffee. A moment for my mind to rest and rejuvenate. My psychologists often told me that I needed to take a few moments for myself, which I had always refused to do. I could never have imagined that on the one day I decided to take that moment, my son would die. That I would live with the guilt for eternity.

I often rewound time in my head, saw Ben in the coffee shop with me. He sat in the high chair beside me, stuffing muffins in his mouth with a smile, pointing all around us. "Look, Mommy!" he said with his expression, which always seemed to carry an awe of the world surrounding him. We then went on a walk together at the park with my parents. I pushed him in the swing. He was safe. He was happy.

Instead, I sat alone in the coffee shop while he sat alone in my husband's car. He was crying while I was reading. The clink of my spoon against the coffee cup marking off the passage of each moment as he sat alone, waiting to see our faces as we came to get him. What was I doing when he died? Was I sipping from my cup, turning a page, gazing out the window into the bright summer sunlight? I had seen Kyle's car parked on Main Street as I drove the girls to Vacation Bible School. *Wow you dropped Ben off fast,* I could have texted him. Or, *how was drop-off?* as I ritualistically asked each morning walking into my office. But not that day. *I see your car,* I texted instead. It was unusual, but I continued driving. *I must have mistaken the time he left home,* I thought. I had passed him by as Ben sat quietly, waiting to be taken to daycare. He texted me when he arrived at work. I had just parked at the coffee shop. *We'll board the dog while your parents are in town with theirs,* he told me. That morning our household had been too busy, we both agreed. We talked about everything but Ben, who we knew was safe and sound, where he should have been, at daycare, playing, smiling.

I had taken the girls by Kyle's office at lunch to surprise him with an early afternoon hello. Riley had jumped out of the car to run and hug him. I had sat feet from where Ben lay. I was oblivious, as the moments passed and we continued living. I did not know, in an instant, it could all be gone.

For Kyle, the guilt would never be satiated. The morning had been typical for our family. I awoke to the sound of activity in the kitchen below, the clank of bowls and spoons. We scurried about as I rushed the girls along in their preparation for Vacation Bible School. Cereal. Clothes. Brush your teeth. Kyle brought Ben into my bathroom, where I stood washing my face. Ruffled hair and wrinkled pajamas from a good night's sleep, puffy face not ready to be woken. Kyle carried him on his hip. Ben looked at me as I stepped closer. Disheveled hair fell down into his eyes. I brushed it back, "You're too pretty to be a boy," I had said. He pushed me away, in his independent way, and I kissed his leg anyway. Had I said I love you? I am sure I did. Or did he leave without my telling him? I'd thought I had more time with him. There was always more time.

I heard giggles as Kyle laid him on the bed, blowing raspberries on his stomach. As I rushed through the kitchen minutes later, Ben sat on Kyle's lap eating oatmeal and yogurt. Kyle flew the spoon into his mouth like an airplane, and Ben smirked.

"Girls, hurry up," I prodded them. "Brush your teeth."

My mother was cleaning up the dishes, my father walking our dog outside.

"Dad, please leave the dog alone for now," I had said, standing on the side porch. "You are going to hurt your back lifting the pen to clean it."

Kyle put Ben in the car and walked up to join me. "I'll take care of the dog tomorrow," he had said. "He doesn't have to do this."

"Fine," I responded. He got into the car and backed up in a rush. I stood by the front window, watching him leave. Dust flew beneath his tires. "We've got to go. You're going to be late," I had relayed to the girls upstairs a few minutes later as we followed him out.

Less than a mile down the road, he missed the left turn, which he took each and every day, school or daycare. An instant that will continue to stand between us for a lifetime. A half a mile further, he then sat at a stop sign at the end of the road, waiting for cars to pass. His habitual memory told him, here, with this stop sign on your right, house across the street with white picket fence, here is where you always turn right. To work, to town, to coffee, to the park, to the grocery store. You are never here, needing to turn left. Left goes nowhere. It was a small town. A habit had already formed. His hands turned the car to the right instead of left, and from that moment onward, the impossible unfolded.

We would struggle with that day for eternity. Whether I could blame but still forgive. Whether we could feel guilt and still survive. Guilt was not an adequate descriptor for that day. It was the peeling away of the soul, into time, into space, becoming nothing but a dark abyss of regret.

93

The smell of suntan lotion. The sound of splashing, children laughing. A steady inundation of summer heat broken periodically by a gentle breeze. I opened my eyes. A mother rocking her son beneath the tree to my left, and his navy bathing suit. A flash of adrenaline raced through my body as I sat up in the lounge chair searching for the girls in the pool.

Yet, in my mind, I am not in Colorado. I am at our beach in Ridgefield. Ben is sitting in the sand before me, navy bathing suit and hat, throwing a ball, laughing, crawling to pick it up again. The girls are off to the side playing soccer in the sand with friends. There is laughter. Kayaks glide across the lake. Our friends surround us, the hum of talking, and a comfort, which soon turns rough and raw as they all dissolve around me. They are gone, and I find myself sitting again on a lounge chair in Colorado without Ben.

"I don't know what's happening," I told a friend on the phone. "I was here and then I was in Connecticut. It was last summer. I miss it. I miss Ben. I miss everything." I was shaking and anxious.

"I know. We feel it here too," she said. "As the summer started getting warmer ... we are having a hard time too. We miss you."

"What do I do?" I asked.

"I don't know. I really don't. I'm sorry," she whispered.

Flashbacks began to appear more often as the summer progressed, and I allowed them to occur. I became mired in memories from the past, which only led to more frequent breakdowns and depression. I relived the feelings of sudden loss. The instant that hangs tremulously in the balance. Ben is dead. Repeatedly. We are moving, and the moment is gone. Just out of my grasp, evanescent and delicate. I began to fear more loss, which meant I then feared everything. I feared loving again or being loved. I avoided life and retreated into myself. Several friends asked me why I refused to look into their eyes when I talked to them. I had not been like that before I knew death. I avoided the connection in eye contact. As if by looking into my eyes, they could see what I had seen, felt what I had felt. It would mean I could connect with another person, let them in, something which I was determined to avoid.

94

The sultry sound of blues music echoed beneath the bridge in mid-July. Kyle and I sat off to the side in our folding chairs with friends. The crowd of hundreds swelled out of their seats and onto the dance floor at the foot of the stage. Deep tides of sound swept through my body as the band sang a rendition of "A Change Is Gonna Come." Tears formed, and I wiped them away. Undulations of emotion matched the rise and fall of the music. Our friends tried not to look as I cried. They hadn't known us back then. They could not unwrap my emotions and peer underneath, even if they wanted to. I stood and walked to the back of the venue to be alone. I missed Ben; I missed my life. *I need change. Please bring change,* I thought.

As the night ended, we told our friends goodbye. We would stay for awhile. I had begged Kyle to go out with me, dancing downtown, anything other than to take me home. I needed something that sleep would not bring. I needed to feel alive again, to feel something other than sorrow and longing. We were taking time off from work to heal in Colorado as I drifted off each evening in a slumber induced by anti-anxiety medications while struggling each weekend to fill in the void left by Ben's death, whether by alcohol or time with friends who could keep our minds busy. I was determined to prove I could be fun again, not a downer, that happiness was possible. I was just going about it in the wrong way. I was lost and floundering with no real hope of recovery.

Later that night, I looked around me as we danced and felt as if I were in an unknown world. Smoke floating up from the floorboards. Dancers on stages around us. The faces of the crowd, blank and foreign. Meaningless. I drifted in a sea of movement that swelled and heaved. Music pounding from the speakers, a drink in my hand. We were not finding happiness; we were finding nothingness. Emptiness. As we tumbled home around one o'clock in the morning, munching on cold pizza, I felt an uncomfortable ache in my chest.

"I don't know who I am anymore. I'm not real. I'm filling a void," I told Kyle.

He nodded his head, insinuating he understood.

"I'll never be able to put myself in your position, but I've tried to understand what you are going through. Can you do that for me?" I questioned him. I needed relief, and I needed it quickly.

"Don't you get it?" my voice escalated. "I didn't choose this." Waving my arms around, gesticulating toward the house, the city, the world. "Overnight I was uprooted from my entire life and implanted in a foreign land. I was happy there, and so were the girls. I miss home. I miss Ridgefield. The community, our family of friends, picking the girls up from school each day, my colleagues, the park, the restaurants. All of it." I was Dorothy in *The Wizard of Oz*. I was a tree growing in barren land, and the same was true for the girls. They were there, and then overnight, they were gone. Their seats in their classrooms were mysteriously empty; Kaylyn's spot on the soccer field was filled by another. Our seats at the beach club were empty. We had disappeared into the night. Ghosts.

95

I stood with Kaylyn and three of her friends the next Monday, watching the demolition of the old Ballard Park playground in Ridgefield. I had booked a flight at two o'clock Sunday morning. I needed to go home. I had felt the grip of something around my soul, and I had to stave it off.

As the bulldozer razed the slide she had once played on, the other girls jumped up and down shouting, "Wow! This new playground will be so awesome!" Kaylyn, however, crouched on the rock wall. Watching. She turned to me, slowly, with searching eyes. "That's so sad. Why would they do that? It contains so many memories." She was thinking of the hours we had spent as a family on the playground, two-year-old Riley building castles in the sand, Kaylyn running across the wooden suspension bridge.

I did not know how to separate the natural need to mourn what was, to hold onto the memories, from a real dissatisfaction with what existed now. I knew I could not get the past back. I could not re-enter my old life, with Ben still in it and happiness abounding. Life had changed. There was death and guilt and blame. People had moved on, and we were different, but something had changed in Ridgefield. The memories in March had brought only pain, but now they had turned into a comfort of sorts, as if I was able to curl up wrapped in a blanket of memories of us. Maybe it was because I had integrated the events of the prior summer into who I was as a person. The small-town community, the coffee shop, park, library… the people… they had taken pieces of me, and I them, until the lines between us became blurry to the touch. Ben had walked the roads, laughed in Ballard Park, worn his teddy bear Halloween costume on Main Street, cold but grinning. This town knew me, and in that moment, my entire being yearned just for that. To be known, to be understood, to just be me, and the new me included our tragedy. I did not need anonymity anymore. I needed love.

I had become immobile, unsure of which way to move, and was coming undone. By the end of our weeklong visit, I was on edge. A razor-sharp edge. Torn between two worlds and stuck in an invisible void in the middle.

96

I returned to Colorado with a brain of electricity, thoughts flashing in and out of existence. And the darkness. A mass of incoherence. I began self-medicating again, with more friends, more parties. I looked around me at the blank faces, foreign and strange, and I did not care. My newfound antipathy for life was morphing into belligerence when I drank, and as my agitation and depression deepened, I could no longer hide my illness from others. They stood watching with wide eyes as I self-destructed, trying to understand, but they could not. I could not even understand.

I began to realize my breakdowns were not about Ben anymore. They were about me. Ben was the love I could not give to myself, and now it was all gone. I had finally fallen into the deep chasm of pain, fed by denial and self-hatred. I could not pull myself out because I wanted to wallow in its depths. Life had become unworthy of the struggle. I had slowly become disengaged from my own soul, with nowhere to go but further into the darkness.

*****

It was September 17, 2015. I had agreed to attend a ladies' night out with friends. Kyle was the designated driver. I placed my drink on the ledge while we danced the two-step. Drugs were slipped into my drink by a stranger. Hours later, my mind had turned into a muddled pool of consciousness. Nothing was real. I could not tell left from right, and I began to free fall. There were no thoughts, there was no reality, and I became like a caged animal for the last time. I was angry, depressed, and grieving, with my emotions overrun. I tore through the crowd, walking to nowhere, and everyone witnessed it. I could not hold the door open, it slammed into my face. Blood formed in the cut above my right eye. People stared. *Why are they staring?* I had wondered. I had to escape the staring. I had to run. From myself, from the world.

    I stumbled out the front door and heard only the whirring of cars in the distance. I did not even know where I was. I began walking in the direction of the sound. They were whirring fast. My brain had left. My body was failing, but something remained that guided me away from the road. My body was beginning to feel heavy, like lead. I needed to sit. If I sat, I would be safe. I could be found, and I desperately yearned to be found. In that moment, I simply needed to just Be.

97

It is September 24, 2015, and I find myself sitting beneath the aspens. I hear them within me, their bold yellow, tremulous whispers. They sing to me and dance in rhythm. I arrived less than twenty-four hours ago, but I feel as if I have always been here in this moment, listening, and forever will be here, in this form or another, searching for Ben, accepting myself, and finding God. I stood yesterday at Independence Pass, marking the Continental Divide, and wondered whether there really was a distinction between the rocks beneath my feet, my mind that was not quite working properly, his eyes in the bluebird sky, and God. My rational mind has always thought yes, there is. But I hear something else in the rustle above, as if the leaves speak of a different truth, beyond the world before me.

I ran from the world to find Ben here, in the wind tunneling through the valley, mountains rising above me to the clouds, colors emerging yellow orange. However, it was less of a running from the world and more of a falling into myself, into the rust-colored soil, short mountain shrubs, peaks ground through years of silent turmoil, shifting and searching too. As I drove along Highway 82 out of Twin Peaks, I was suddenly overtaken by the color of the aspens that draped above the roadway and felt at home within my own skin for the first time. My brain could not create a rationale for the tears that flowed; I was simply overwhelmed by the beauty of being alive beneath a tapestry of gold. I felt a harmony within myself, a resonance with something greater.

So I sit on this bench alone, existing, breathing, and for now, that is enough to pull life out of death. Ben is all around me. I feel him here, within me. I speak to him. And through him, I have found myself—in the full living vibrancy of the autumn leaves. Some posit that the universe, all this surrounding me, appeared out of nothing, but I know differently now. I have been where nothing should reside and found something there. I found love, a core of myself, which I had never known before, and I found beauty in the simplicity of the living. I am no longer alone, for a wholeness surrounds me, an interdependence of everything, as far as I can see and beyond. This comfort and love, it is God, and through Ben, I know this to be true.

98

Four observation platforms protrude from the ground a few yards from the pond at the Aspen Center for Environmental Studies. Each day, I place my folding chair beneath the aspens at the back of the highest platform, where I can sit partially hidden from hikers who pass now and again by the edge of the water. I feel the sun against my back, adding warmth to the days which are already beginning to turn chilly. Bluebirds dance from branch to branch. I admire their acrobatics. An eight-point buck lies beneath a tree about six feet behind me, calm and observant. His mate eventually comes to meet him, and they walk off through the brush. He had been waiting for her to return too.

I have escaped, but for the last time. I have finally fallen into myself, where I have longed to be for so many years. Four days on the new medication, and it is already beginning to work. My frenzied mind has slowed to a rhythmic crawl, smooth and unflustered. I can think clearly about the past, of Ben and losing him, and the future, of what I want that to be. I can feel the pain of the loss and its aftermath, allowing it to flow like a river through my body without getting snagged on the branches and turn toward some form of hope ahead. I feel as if I am one with nature, the bluebirds flitting about, hills rising above, deer trotting through the tall grass. But most importantly, I have come full circle and found myself. Beneath the aspens. I find a comfort in being the only person I can be in this one moment. I have found beauty in the imperfection of it all. Of life and love. I have a mental illness, but I am worthy of love and acceptance just as I am. A mother, wife, friend, attorney. I am all of those things. There is a relief in not hiding anymore. A relief in being free.

99

"Something is different about you, Mom," Kaylyn says to me a few weeks after my return home from Aspen. The three of us are sitting in an examination room at an urgent care, waiting for doctors to check Kaylyn's ear for a possible infection. Riley had just sat on my lap in the waiting room, engrossed in silly repartee with the television. I had tickled her ribs, and we both emitted wholesome belly laughs, rocking back and forth. I held her tightly.

"What's different?" I respond out of curiosity.

"You laugh a lot more now," she says, leaning back on her elbows atop the exam table. "You seem happier."

It startles me to understand how scarred my interactions with the world, even friends and family, have been, but it comforts me to see how easily the bridges can be mended. Sometimes it was as simple as a laugh here and there. A smile. The medication my doctor had given me was newly approved for treatment of bipolar depression, and the only side effect that had worried us was high blood sugar, a side effect that had plagued me in the past. I prayed, talked to Ben, to God, before checking my glucose levels in Aspen. I felt as if my entire future depended on finding at least one medication that worked without side effects, and as I read the number on the monitor, a tsunami of relief washed over me. There was hope.

I often think of all the mistakes I have made in my life, the ramifications of self-denial, of struggling with a mental illness and striving for perfection, and I know I never want to go back. I have to find the space to forgive myself and move on. To throw away the chains and start anew. I have seen rock bottom and found love there. A love of life, of others, and finally, of myself. So I have to make the most of my second chance. I have to live, and as I look at Kaylyn across the room, our eyes meet with a smile. I know just where to begin.

100

"'I know who I am!'" the Little Soul says.[25] I look into my daughters' eyes as I read to them. Their fingers trace the glossy pages of the book lying before us on the bed.

"'I'm the Light!'" A little angel stands atop fluffy clouds, looking into the sky of yellow and orange.

"'But soon, knowing who it was, was not enough. The Little Soul felt stirrings inside, and now wanted to *be* who it was.'" They watch me intently, eyes big and questioning.

"'There is nothing else *but* the Light,' God tells him, 'since you cannot see yourself as the Light when you are *in* the Light, we'll surround you with darkness.'"

"See, girls, in order to know anything, you have to understand its opposite. You cannot know what it is to be truly happy without knowing sadness," I explain to them. They nod their heads.

"'I want to be the part of *special* called "forgiving",' the Little Soul says, 'I want to experience myself as that.' Yet there is no one to forgive, for all the other little souls are the Light too, so God must find a soul to partner with him, a Friendly Soul, to go into darkness, to give the Little Soul something to forgive."

"'Why would you do that for me?'" the Little Soul asks the Friendly Soul.

"'I would do it because I love you,'" the Friendly Soul replies. The Little Soul looks surprised.

"'Don't be so amazed,' the Friendly Soul continues. 'You have done the same thing for me. Don't you remember? Oh, we have danced together, you and I, many times. Through the eons and across all the ages have we danced.'"

"'Thus have we come together, you and I, many times before; *each* bringing to the *other* the exact and perfect opportunity to express and to experience who we really are.'"

I turn the page, as they examine the fog of darkness, both souls slipping into the garments of physical existence. "'I have but one favor to ask of you in return,' says the Friendly Soul. 'In the moment that I do the worst to you that you could possibly imagine... Remember Who I Really Am.'"

*****

As I sit across from Kyle on the ottoman of our couch, I think back to the feelings of sadness I experienced on my recent trip to Connecticut. A sense of chronic yearning for what was. A past that was gone, with only the future lying ahead. A new, frightening future.

"I don't know how to get past it," I tell him, knowing this will be hard for him to hear, "what happened that day." I pause, examining his face, which he holds at a downward slant, as if watching the floor shift and crack beneath him. "Maybe we need couples therapy, or more time together, just us. I need to hear you say it was your fault, and why, and admit you took our lives away." I could not get past the helplessness I felt the day Ben died, of having him taken away in an instant, without any act of my own.

"I've never said anything but the fact that it was my fault. It was all my fault," he states, avoiding my eyes. "I live with it every day. Sometimes I have so much guilt it makes me not want to be alive anymore." He looks up, as if uncovering something important.

"I don't understand these feelings I have. They scare me. My love for you, it's changed, it's different, and I don't know how to move forward." I need help navigating our new world.

"I understand," he looks down again, a weight on his shoulders.

"What happened that day," I glance away, into the kitchen, at nothing. "What happened… You are so…" I pause, searching for the right word. "Flawed."

Immediately, that one word triggers an avalanche within my soul, for I understand instantaneously with its utterance. I myself am utterly flawed too. I visualize those dark nights of my past, Kyle running his hands through my tangled hair. "You will be okay. We will get through this," he would tell me in a whisper. "I love you." We have always been two souls dancing together through the eons, learning through living, who we are. Understanding joy through pain. Learning forgiveness through tragedy. Carrying each other out of the darkness and into the light. We are soul partners, and I finally see. That core of love, of God, which has ushered us through the night, it is something worth fighting for.

101

I snap a picture of the girls in front of the *Star Wars* advertisement in the lobby of the movie theater. Riley has a Cheshire Cat grin, missing her two front teeth, 3D movie glasses sitting atop her nose. Kaylyn stands beside her, more mature in stature with a slight grin on her face, left knee bent like she is a teenager already. Kyle is saving our seats while we move on to play air hockey together. I win by one, as the puck forcefully falls into the tiny slit.

"Noooo," Kaylyn yells with a smile.

"Alright, let's get to our seats for the movie," I say, watching the girls skip down the hall to join their father.

As the movie begins, I can sense their excitement sitting in silence, adjusting their glasses. Riley leans closer to me, snuggling up beneath my arm, which I rest by her side, but that is not enough for her. She gently takes my hand and wraps it around her waist. She wants to snuggle more closely. She needs to feel my touch.

It is my birthday, December 21, 2015. I think about Christmas, which will soon arrive, the second since Ben's death. It has been a lonely season, but we have finally been able to fall into the comfort of each other again. Nights spent cooking in the kitchen, Christmas tree lit, music playing. Each day we eat dinner as a family at the kitchen table and then play a game of Bellz® before moving to the couch to watch a Christmas movie together.

I look at Kaylyn sitting two seats away from me. Her legs are pulled up to her chest, hand on her face as she watches the movie. We still pretend Santa Claus visits, even though both girls are getting older and most likely know the truth. Some parents may fault me for pretending a magical old man exists who flies across the globe in one night, delivering presents to all the children of the world. Yet I don't feel guilty. I need her to have a bit more time to enjoy the innocence and joy of childhood. The realities of adult life will greet her all too soon. I see now that I have succeeded. I lean back in my chair, content.

When Riley finally moves back onto her own seat, Kyle looks at me beneath his glasses and gives me a peck on the lips while taking my hand. I have realized that it is possible to fall in love with someone more than once. Over and over again, as many times as needed. It begins in the stillness of the night as you sit on the couch together watching reruns. Then it grows and morphs. You are laughing over dinner. You are holding hands in a movie theater. True love isn't meant to be easy or superficial. Sometimes it is rough and dirty. Other times it is gentle and comforting. But it is always there, waiting to be rediscovered.

Epilogue

I pick up the photograph, turn it over in my hand, and run my fingers along the edges, curled up at the corners. I blow the dust off the surface, wiping it with the arm of my sweater. A man and woman stand together on a sandy shore. He places his arm around her waist. Both smile, eyes squinting in the summer sun reflecting off the water. The world is before them, and time, so much time. I am trying to remember those days, but it is only the vestige of an old world I no longer know. It is an antiquated vision, but comforting. Part of me wants to live like that again. To know my place in the world. A defined world that is understandable. Where there is a real right or wrong, love or hate, forgiveness or blame. A categorized life, neat and tidy. But I live in that world no more. The leather box from which it came lies splayed open on the desk before me. I gently place the photograph on the red velvet surface inside and close the golden clasp. I tiptoe to return the box to the top shelf of our closet. Safely out of reach.

Our experience changed me. So much pain, yet so much love. I saw the best of humanity and the worst of humanity in such a short period of time. I no longer see the world in black and white. It is the gray of charcoal drawn on a canvas before me, black blurring into a cloudy shadow turning white. One or the other, both and neither at once. I no longer believe things are as they appear on the surface, with events or people. I do not judge others before I try to uncover what lies beneath.

I want to know that part. The real part. The love and the pain. And not just with people, with the world around me as well.

I have often heard people say God is compassion. I disagree in part. He is more than that. God is empathy. The projection of your pain, love, struggles onto me such that I become infused with it—merged with it. So that I can try to understand, be sensitive to, experience you. So that I can experience a very human love. God is the blurring of one body into the next until they become one—the charcoal gray. That is the world I want to live in. Without that, there is only isolation and pain.

I debated the pros and cons of publishing this book for eight years, scared of the repercussions of coming out as a professional with a mental illness. However, I realized I yearned to be free, and I had a right to be free. I had a right to perform at a high level as a career professional, raise my children, be a strong wife to a husband who needed me, and also talk openly about mental illness in society. I want to empower others to do the same. To disrupt the dialogue around mental illness in society. My mental illness is one part of me, but it does not define me. This book is Ben's voice, as he saved me and gave me the strength to speak out. And that is the love of a son for his mother.

This memoir was written in the throes of emotion in the fall of 2015, and since then, life has been nothing near perfect. It has been an epic journey of self-discovery and finding life's purpose through examination of my heart and soul. There is so much more that comes… after survival.

Mental Health Resources

Almost fifty-three million adults in America suffer from a mental illness, often in isolation and shame. This represents one in five adults. Almost 20.8 percent of the homeless are experiencing a serious mental health condition, and 37 percent of imprisoned adults have a diagnosed mental illness. Ninety percent of those who commit suicide each year have shown symptoms of an underlying mental illness. Suicide is the second leading cause of death among people age ten to fourteen and the third leading cause of death among people age fifteen to twenty-four in the U.S. The cumulative effect on productivity and lost income in America due to mental illness is estimated to be nearly $193 billion.

The lasting effects of keeping mental illness shrouded in secrecy, not only on individuals and their families but society as a whole, are immeasurable. If you believe you or a loved one has a mental illness and needs help, you can find resources. Suicide is never a solution. People and support systems are here to help. Here are just a few organizations that are able and willing to point you in the right direction:

National Alliance on Mental Illness
http://nami.org
Helpline: 800-950-6264, Text: 62640
Email: helpline@nami.org

National Suicide Prevention Lifeline
1-800-273-TALK (8255)

SAMHSA Treatment Referral Hotline
1-800-662-HELP (4357)

Acknowledgments

Thank you endlessly to all of the practitioners who helped me through my struggles over the years.

Thank you to my parents. Without your love and support, I would never have the courage to be myself and go public with our story.

Deepest thanks to all of my friends who supported me through the tragedy and beyond. In addition, I am truly grateful for Peter Buzaid and John Robert Gulash, who guided us through the legal inroads of our journey.

A very special thank you to Wellness Writers Press and my publishers, Julie Colvin and Leila Summers, who believed in me and made my dreams come true.

Thank you to my publicists at High10 Media for their support in getting my message out.

Many thanks to Janette Fennell and Amber Rollins at Kids and Car Safety, who helped me through every step of our tragedy, as well as Senators Blumenthal and Murphy.

Most sincere thank you to my dear husband, Kyle, without whom I would not be here today. Your love and unwavering support have gotten me through the darkest days. You are my soulmate. To my daughters, Kaylyn and Riley, as without you I would not be complete. You are the light in my life.

Always and forever, thank you, Ben, for bringing me back to myself and giving me a voice with which to speak out. I love you endlessly.

Notes

1 French, Karen L. *The Hidden Geometry of Life: The Science and Spirituality of Nature*. London: Watkins Media Limited, 2014.

2 Hemingway, Ernest. *A Farewell to Arms*. New York: Scribner Classics, 1997.

3 Birmaher, Boris and Kelly Monk. "Bios Family Study," *Child and Adolescent Bipolar Spectrum Services, University of Pittsburgh*. Accessed January 30, 2022. https://www.pediatricbipolar.pitt.edu/research/bios-family-study.

4 Frankl, Viktor E. *Man's Search for Meaning*. Boston: Beacon Press, 2006.

5 The decision to prosecute caregivers is often fact-specific and dependent upon the prosecutors who are handling each case. For instance, prosecution rates would be higher for caregivers who intentionally decide to leave their child in a car or where there are other incriminating circumstances, such as drug use. According to Kids and Car Safety, from 1990–2020, at least 52 percent of child hot car deaths resulted in no criminal conviction. In 44 percent of cases, no criminal charges were ever filed and in 8 percent of cases, all charges were dropped. Only 31 percent of cases result in a conviction with varying degrees, and those convicted rarely serve any jail time. "Child Hot Car Deaths Data Analysis - Kidsandcars.org."

U.S. Child Hot Car Death Data Analysis from the Kids and Car Safety National Database 2.2022. Kids and Car Safety. Accessed January 22, 2023. http://www.kidsandcars.org/wp-content/uploads/2020/07/Child-Hot-Car-Deaths-Data-Analysis.pdf.

6   National Highway Traffic Safety Administration (NHTSA) Not-In-Traffic Surveillance data shows that hyperthermia (heatstroke) is the number-one cause of death in non-crash fatalities for children under the age of fifteen. US Department OF Transportation. "TFFIC SFT FCTS - noheatstroke.org." Research Note: Not-in-Traffic Surveillance: Non-Crash Fatalities and Injuries. NHTSA'S National Center for Statistics and Analysis, March 2015. https://www.noheatstroke.org/NHTSA2015.pdf.

Between 1990 and 2020, there were a total of 994 fatalities from heatstroke in vehicles. The average number of heat stroke deaths per year is thirty-nine, with a high of fifty-four in 2018 alone. Data shows that the majority (55 percent) of vehicle heatstroke deaths are caused by a caregiver accidentally leaving the child in a vehicle. "Child Hot Car Dangers Fact Sheet - Kidsandcars.org." Heatstroke-fact-sheet. Kids and Car Safety. Accessed January 22, 2023. https://www.kidsandcars.org/wp-content/uploads/2020/01/Heatstroke-fact-sheet.pdf.

So-called "hot car deaths" have been highly politicized for over two decades. General Motors issued a press release in 2001 stating that it was moving quickly to address this serious safety problem, calling hot car deaths totally preventable. Since then, safety advocates and politicians have battled for legislation either requiring driver notification systems in cars or requiring more government-sponsored research into the prevention of hot car deaths. On July 6, 2012, President Obama signed into law the Moving Ahead for Progress in the Twenty-First Century Act (MAP-21), which allowed the Department of Transportation to initiate safety research into the viability of vehicle technology and public awareness campaigns to minimize hyperthermia deaths occurring each year.

After Ben's death and other instances of children being left in cars in the State of Connecticut earlier that summer, Senators Blumenthal and Murphy sent a letter to the then-Acting Administrator of NHTSA, David Friedman, asking that more resources be directed to public awareness campaigns in the state. Thirty-two children died from hyperthermia in cars in 2014, including a high-profile case in Georgia, heightening awareness of these tragedies in the public eye that summer. In the aftermath of our loss, Kyle and I knew we could not get our son back; however, we felt it may be possible to join with other safety advocates and try to raise awareness to prevent future deaths.

We made the decision to go public and, with Janette Fennell, founder and president of Kids and Car Safety, met with several Congressmen and David Friedman of NHTSA during our trip to Washington, DC. Our goal was to open a dialogue of all issues surrounding hot car deaths and raise awareness of the risks of hyperthermia in vehicles as well as put a face to these tragedies, which are often sensationalized in the media. We believe there is no one way or right way to prevent hot car deaths. It is a complicated combination of personal accountability, public awareness, and research into potential technological solutions, but it is an important dialogue in the child safety arena that has been going on for years and should continue.

In November 2021, the Hot Cars Act, part of the Infrastructure Bill, was signed into law by President Biden. The version of the Hot Cars Act passed by the US House of Representatives and Senate requires NHTSA to issue a final rule requiring car manufacturers to equip cars with a system to alert the operator to check rear-designated seating positions after the vehicle engine or motor is deactivated by the operator. The bill does not require car manufacturers to install devices to sense if a child is left in the backseat after the vehicle engine or motor is deactivated by the operator.

7   The DCF record reviewed for this memoir contains reports of my mental illness by an emergency room nurse and our family pediatrician, though

no mention of its effect on my ability to care for my children were made or insinuated by the two parties. To the contrary, our pediatrician and my psychiatrist made verbal or written statements concerning my ability to manage my mental illness and care for my children. The record indicates "Ms. Seitz had informed [pediatrician] that she has history of Bipolar D/O, has a strong family history of such and has been medicated, was off the meds for part of the last pregnancy, and has remained stable for years."

The record and petition claim "diagnosis of Bipolar, previous diagnosis of Post-Partum Depression and instability." The report made to Colorado CPS states that "Lindsey has a history of bipolar, and she has been in treatment since she was a teenager. Lindsey has a history of making poor choices as a result of her bipolar. Lindsey is supposed to be medicated, but [reporting party] is not sure if she is taking medication." Contents of the report to Colorado CPS remain unsubstantiated, since, for instance, I was not diagnosed as a teenager with any mental illness, instead only receiving a diagnosis in my early twenties. No concern was raised over my coping mechanisms or ability to care for my children. To my knowledge, no efforts were made to substantiate the truth of any of the above-mentioned claims.

8 My accounts of drug side effects in this memoir are based on personal experience only and are often the result of the fact that certain antidepressants are not meant for use in those with bipolar disorder due to exacerbation of manic episodes. Consult package inserts and manufacturer websites for more information.

9 Kyle had disclosed the fact that he was seeing a psychotherapist on a bi-weekly basis and was being treated with antidepressants by our family practitioner. He did not sign a full consent for DCF to speak with his psychotherapist or to access his full psychotherapy records, which would contain private details of his grieving process and details of the day his son died.

10   Under Connecticut law, DCF must obtain consent for an interview from a child's parent unless DCF has reason to believe such person is the perpetrator of alleged abuse. Conn. Gen. Stat. § 17a-101(h) (2020). Absent consent, DCF must seek a court order and show evidence that an interview is warranted and in the best interest of the child.

11   My attorney was referring to what scholars call "defensive social work." It is rooted in an unjust placement of blame on the child protective agencies for the cases of child abuse, neglect, or even death that are spattered as headlines on local newspapers on an almost daily basis. Many child protective services personnel base decisions on fear, "fear of job discipline, fear of civil (and even criminal) liability, and especially fear of adverse publicity resulting from the death of a child." Chill, Paul. "Burden of Proof Begone: The Pernicious Effect of Emergency Removal in Child Protective Proceedings." *Family Court Review* 42, no. 3 (2004): 542. Besharov, Douglas J., and Susan H. Besharov. "Teaching About Liability." *Social Work* 32, no. 6 (1987): 517–22.

According to Professor Douglas Besharov, the first director of the US National Center on Child Abuse and Neglect, "[Child protective agencies] are under great pressure to take no chances, and to intervene whenever they might be criticized for not doing so. The dynamic is simple enough: negative media publicity—and a lawsuit—is always possible if the child is subsequently killed or injured; but there will be no critical publicity if it turns out that intervention was unneeded. (And how could people tell anyway?)" Besharov, Douglas J. "Protecting Abused and Neglected Children: Can Law Help Social Work? *Child Abuse and Neglect* 7, no. 4 (1983): 424.

Many possible solutions have been presented to quell the need for defensive social work, which can have such negative consequences on children and families. Besharov suggests a systemic change, which would reflect the realities of child protective decision-making as it is impossible for even the best caseworker to predict the future maltreatment of a child, and the fact that he or she should not be blamed for failing to do so. For example, adjusting the basis for protective action, relating it to certain behavior on the part of a parent that can be more logically connected to future risk to children in a statistically significant way. Protective action would be warranted if a parent has engaged in abusive or neglectful behavior in the past, either resulting in injury or whose reasonably foreseeable consequence could have been serious injury. Also, he suggests the authorization of intervention only after clear and sufficient proof of the need to do so. In addition, experts point out the need for a more realistic approach to covering child protection cases in the media and better educating the public on related issues in order to take unnecessary and unrealistic pressure off child services agencies. Harris, Nigel. "Defensive Social Work." *Br. J. Social Work* 17, no. 1 (1987): 61–69. Ayre, Patrick. "Child Protection and the Media: Lessons from the Last Three Decades." *Br. J. Social Work* 31, no. 6 (2001): 887–901.

12 Otto, Rudolf. *The Idea of the Holy: An Inquiry Into the Non-Rational Factor in the Idea of the Divine and Its Relation to the Rational.* Columbia: Pantianos Classics, 1923.

13 Emerson, Ralph Waldo. *Nature*. Boston: James Munroe and Company, 1836.

14 Plato, translated by Desmond Lee. *The Republic*. New York: Penguin Group, 1974.

15 Huxley, Aldous. *The Perennial Philosophy*. New York: HarperCollins Publishers, 1945.

16 Rinpoche, Sogyal. *The Tibetan Book of Living and Dying*. San Francisco: HarperSanFrancisco, 2020.

17 Ibid.

18 Alexander, Eben. *The Map of Heaven: How Science, Religion, and Ordinary People Are Proving the Afterlife*. New York: Simon & Schuster, 2014.

19 Capra, Fritjof. "Foreword" in Berendt, Joachim-Earnst. *The World Is Sound: Nada Brahma: Music and the Landscape of Consciousness*. Rochester, Vermon: Destiny Books, 1991.

20 Cook, Francis. *Hua-Yen Buddhism: The Jewel Net of Indra*. State College, Pennsylvania: Penn State Press, 1977.

21 Scholars in the field often discuss the psychological and emotional trauma resulting not only from the removal of children from their homes but also from the mere insertion of the agency's quasi-police authority into the private sphere of a family's life. Children are surrounded by complete strangers, inserted into foreign environments, often separated from the only family and safety they know. "Failure to act may lead to a child's serious injury or death… On the other hand, intervening when a child is not in danger can leave lasting psychological scars on the child as well as the parents," states Besharov. Besharov, Douglas J. "Protecting Abused and Neglected Children: Can Law Help Social Work? *Child Abuse and Neglect* 7, no. 4 (1983): 424.

Akka Gordon, a former investigator for New York City's Administration for Children's Services, describes her experience on a typical night in the Emergency Children Services building in Soho, in which thirty to forty children who have been removed from their families are brought in:

"When children first arrive at ECS they are taken through a metal detector by security. Some carry garbage bags containing their clothes; others tightly clutch just the one item they brought from home… Some of these kids, who range from newborn babies to 17-year-olds have been rescued from seriously abusive or neglectful parents. Others are here for reasons that are ambiguous, unjustified, even arbitrary… And because the city's Administration for Children's Services has identified them as children in danger, this is the first of many unfamiliar places they'll be seeing as they journey through the city's foster care system… When I first started coming to ECS, I tried to reach out to all the children who were crying or sitting alone, shocked and terrified. It was easier with the little ones, because I could hug them and they would immediately respond. But the older ones were different… To the manager at ACS who makes the fateful decision to remove a child, and to the judge who approves it, a child exists on a piece of paper, alongside a list of disturbing circumstances. They don't see the child having a panic attack at 3 a.m. because he is suddenly alone in the world. Or slamming his head against a wall out of protest and desperation." Gordon, Akka. "Taking Liberties," *City Limits Monthly*, December 1, 2000. http://citylimits.org/2000/12/01/taking-liberties.

Professor Paul Chill, Associate Dean for Clinical and Experiential Education at the University of Connecticut School of Law and scholar on child protection, suggests several changes to the child protective services system in order to reduce the number of unnecessary removals of children from their homes. A clarification and tightening of the standard of "imminent danger" required for emergency removals, a limitation of the circumstances under which unilateral removals of children without an ex parte court order can be affected, and a strengthening of the ability of parents to offer informal input to the courts. Other scholars propose a stronger focus on the importance of retaining the family unit and its autonomy in child protective cases as well as lessening the adversarial nature of the family-child protective services relationship, therefore offering more room for compromise and negotiation. Sinden, Amy. "Why Won't Mom Cooperate? A Critique of Informality in Child Welfare Proceedings." *Yale Journal of Law & Feminism* 11, no. 2 (1999): 381.

22 Williams, Margery. *The Velveteen Rabbit*. New York: George H. Doran Company, 1922.

23 Holmes, Ernest. *The Science of Mind: A Philosophy, a Faith, a Way of Life* (the Definitive edition). New York: Penguin, 1998.

24 Powers, John. "Naomi Klein on *This Changes Everything*, Her New Book About Climate Change," *Vogue,* August 26, 2014.

25 Walsch, Neale Donald. *The Little Soul and the Sun: A Children's Parable Adapted from Conversations with God.* San Francisco: Hampton Roads Publishing, 1998.

Made in United States
North Haven, CT
08 May 2023